Keys to Open Your Heart – Voume 2

Inspirational and Motivational Illustrations

Based on the Radio Program

"Today's Key to Confident Living"

By

Bill Hossler

Key Publishing Inc.
821 River Oak Run, Fort Wayne, IN 46804
1-888-333-KEYS (5397)
E-Mail: keys@todayskey.net
Visit our Web Page: www.todayskey.net

Also available from Key Publishing, Inc.

Radical Promises for Desperate Times – How God Gets Us Through by Bill Hossler

Keys to Open Your Heart – A Journaling Guide for Men and Women - Book 1 by Bill Hossler

Spenser Rose Is Born – God Planned Me from the Beginning by Margaret Hossler – A children's book.

Editing and Design by Hossler Creative Design
823 Kelsey St. Grand Rapids, MI
www.hosslercreative.com
jim@hosslercreative.com
www.Hosslercreative.com
Phone: 606-706-6947
Cover Design by Jim Hossler

ISBN: 978-0-9650491-7-7

TABLE OF CONTENTS

DEDICATON

      Three men – Kris Overly, Larry Boulier and Marty Doorn – have been of inestimable help to me in the last 20 years of Today's Key to Confident Living radio ministry. Without their financial assistance, technical expertise and encouragement this work would not have continued. I am not with them often, but when I am we are able to pick up where we left off and I always come away renewed and reenergized. Thanks men.

PREFACE

My work with people convinced me a long time ago that many individuals long for some kind of motivational and inspirational thought for the day. Many of these people are not necessarily deeply religious, but they still have high values. They desire to have a time during each day when they are challenged to live a better and more noble life. Such was my motivation for starting "Today's Key To Confident Living" – a radio program that is now heard on scores of radio stations across the United States.

As the number of stations increased, so did the requests for more and more of the scripts. It was decided to put 100 of the scripts into book form. This is now the second book of these scripts.

I trust Keys To Open Your Heart Vol 2 will become one means for unlocking the potential God has given you.
Because of Him,
Bill Hossler

#1 - HONESTY

On her way home from work a woman stopped at the local deli to pick up some chicken for supper. The butcher reached into the barrel where the chickens were kept and pulled out the last one. He put it on the scales and told the lady the weight. The woman thought for a moment and said she needed one just slightly larger. He put the lone chicken back into the barrel and gave the appearance of searching for another one that was just slightly larger. He pulled the same chicken out and told her this one weighed one pound more. She pondered her decision for a moment and then said, "I'll take both of them."

Honesty is still the best policy. Honesty is a virtue that needs to be rekindled in American life. The Bible reminds new converts to the faith that if they had formerly been dishonest they were to cease such activity and speak the truth with one another. One of the most severe judgments in the early church was meted out to a couple who thought they could lie to the Holy Spirit and deceive the church about their actions. God is a God of truth and therefore, to be like Him we also must be people of truthfulness.

Our society foundations are built on honesty. Such honesty affects the success of our marriages, the effectiveness of government, the working relations between labor and management, and most others enterprises. God gave us simple laws to liberate us: laws that can free us from fears, suspicions and cynicism. Honesty when practiced indeed sets us free.

#2 - DAILY DISCIPLINES

Duffy Daugherty was the head football coach at Michigan State University when Dave Kaiser kicked the winning field goal against UCLA. The field goal gave the Spartans a 17-14 margin of victory.

Daugherty noticed that when Kaiser kicked the ball he did not watch it go through the goal posts. When Kaiser came back to the bench, Daugherty mentioned this fact to him. Kaiser commented that he hadn't watched the goal posts because he couldn't see them. He had to watch the referee to see how he would call it. He had left his contact lenses back at the hotel.

Feelings of shock and anger at first came over the coach, but the more he thought about it the more he calmed down. Were the contacts that important? Hadn't his kicker practiced day after day for hours at a time from every conceivable angle on the field? Didn't he know where the goal posts were without even being able to see them? It was the daily disciplines of practice that had made the difference when the football sailed through the uprights.

Our continued attention to the Christian disciplines of moral behavior will also help us in pressure packed situations. If Godly living is a normal practice for us then times of moral testing will not cause us to crumble and fall.

#3 - CLEANING OUT STUFF

In his book <u>Maverick</u>, Recardo Semler tells of a lesson he learned working at Semco. The company was in one of those departmental budget meetings when the subjects of filing cabinets came up. Several departments had been waiting for months to get the badly needed cabinets. When the cost of this budget item alone was tabulated the total came to $50,000.00. Were all the filing cabinets necessary? Did all the paper have to be kept? Semler tells about how they discussed their problem and decided not to buy a single cabinet that day. Instead, they decided to stop the company for half a day and ask every employee to get rid of any unnecessary files - to look inside every file folder and throw out every nonessential piece of paper. It was the First Biannual Semco File Inspection and Clean-out Day.

Selmer was not too sure how the plan would work. His order was in for two additional large file cabinets to go along with the four he already had. But, after the cleanup he was able to get rid of three cabinets he no long needed. His experience was duplicated many times throughout the company. In fact Semco auctioned off dozens of unneeded file cabinets rather than purchasing any.

More important than cleaning out over stuffed file cabinets is the necessity to clean out all the things that keep us from being our best - things that clutter our lives and trip us up. The book of Hebrews says, "let us strip off anything that slows us down or holds us back, and especially those sins that wrap themselves so tightly around our feet and trip us up; and let us run with patience the particular race that God has set before us" (Hebrews 12:1b Living Bible).

#4 - THE WHISPHER TEST

"I grew up knowing I was different, and I hated it," wrote Mary Ann Bird in the **Whisper Test**. A cleft palate, misshapen lip, a nose like a crooked mountainous road, teeth that badly needed braces, speech that was hard to understand and stinging words from my school mates were all a part of her early childhood remembrances.

A birth defect seemed like some horrible kiss of death. Claiming to have had some accident in which the face was badly scarred seemed easier to accept and more understandable on the part of the other students. Love was hard to find. It seemed as those she was destined to live in a lonely world of being ostracized and isolated from those all around her?

However, Mrs. Leonard her second grade teacher, epitomized the value of a word of encouragement. The lifetime power of this short and pleasingly plump teacher's words changed things for Mary Ann. It all happened one day during a routine physical test designed to discover if the children in the classroom could hear OK.

Divine direction from God must have prompted Mrs. Leonard to speak her life changing words to Mary this particular day. The test was simply conducted - no fancy or sophisticated equipment - just the child on one side of the room and the teacher sitting at her desk. Typical phrases used were "The sky is blue" or "Do you have new shoes?" However, for Mary, words for her test were different - they were life changing. She distinctly and clearly heard, "I wish you were my little child." Someone did love her in spite of her physical disfigurement, low self esteem and misunderstood self value? The Whisper Test day was a turning point for Mary.

Today can be a turning point for you. John the Baptist gave those wonderful words of encouragement to everyone when he said, (John 1:12) "to all who received Jesus, to those who believed in His name, he gave the right to become children of God." Jesus says to every one of us, "I wish you were my little child."

#5 - MIDLIFE CRISIS

Is there really a mid life crisis or is it only imaginary and a means of selling books? Most will agree that many men, particularly between the ages of 35 - 50, go through a time of emotional struggle. Serious psychological and physical problems develop for some. Others make dramatic changes in their life styles and revert back to youthful ways and habits. What causes the problem? Is it one of looking at one's own mortality, seeing others pass us by on the road to success, seeing the hopes and dreams we had going unfulfilled or a combination of things?

For some it may be a failed value system that seemed to hold such promise and hope when younger but now appears empty and guilt ridden. The story is told of a man who spent his life climbing the ladder of success only to find that it was leaning against the wrong building. How sad to find that we had lived for the wrong things.

The midway point of one's existence is a good time to re-examine our values and goals. But rather than our discoveries pushing us into childish behavior, hopefully they will cause us to be more involved in those things that will outlive us. The late Jim Elliot, a missionary murdered for his faith, said, "He is no fool who gives what he cannot keep to gain what he cannot lose."

#6 - OVERCOMING ADVERSITY

Adversity can make us either bitter or better. We all know people who have gone through difficult times only to come out refined as sugar with the sweetest and most pleasant outlook on life. Others can go through similar or even less difficulties and turn into grumbling couch potatoes intent on nothing else than one big pity party. But it is in the crucible of trial and testing that some of the great master pieces and works for good and God have been done.

Bunyan wrote *Pilgrim's Progress* from jail. Florence Nightingale, though bed fast because of illness, reorganized the hospitals of England. Pasteur was tireless in his attack on disease, even though he was partially paralyzed and suffered from bouts with loss of consciousness. Francis Parkman, eminent American historian, had such poor eyesight that he could only write a few large words on each page and yet he wrote twenty splendid volumes of history. Handel wrote the great masterpiece, "The Messiah" when he was partially paralyzed and financially broke.

The Apostle Paul, when going through one of his times of testing, received assurance from the Lord that "My grace is sufficient for you, for My power is made perfect in weakness" (2 Corinthians 12:9). Rather than become embittered, Paul said, "I accept my weakness so that the power of Christ may rest on me." Tests and trials are not necessarily pleasant, but they can often do more in us and for us than a life of ease could ever do.

#7 - Serenaded by Birds

Three New Tribe missionaries were held prisoner by Columbian guerrillas. Concerned about their future and the need to feel God's presence one of the prayed for some touch from God similar to what they would give to one of their children. Nothing happened that evening but the next day, Sunday morning, a strange occurrence took place: a whole host of birds came to sing. It was not the usual number of birds but a choir of birds. Some twenty- six classes of birds looked right at the three captives and sang to their hearts content. Rather than flying off after a short while, the birds stayed until 12:00 noon, the time when worship service was normally done. The birds did not return the next day nor the next. They didn't return at all that week but the next Sunday morning they were back in greater number than before and again stayed until noon. What a miracle. It was enough to remind the three of the faithfulness of God and that He had not forgotten them.

You may be going through a time in your life and you wonder if God has forgotten you or even if He knows where you are. He knows and He cares. If He can send a choir of birds to minister to 3 people hidden deep in the Columbian jungle He also knows where you are. He might not answer you in the same way He did the three captives but His presence can be just as comforting.

MAT 6:26 "Look at the birds of the air; they do not sow or reap or store away in barns, and yet your heavenly Father feeds them. Are you not much more valuable than they?"

You are significant to God and He cares for you.

#8 - PRAYING IN TIGHT SPOTS

Have you ever wanted to listen into the prayer line to heaven to hear how people pray especially when they are in tight spots? People in dire circumstances often make vows to God if He will just rescue them and get them out of bad situations. But are those vows kept? Did they really mean them? Or did they only agree to certain things because they were trying to drive a bargain with God and then forget them when the crisis was over?

It is something like the story of two frightened men adrift in an open boat on a stormy lake. Finally, one of the men begins to pray. He didn't know much about prayer, but he knew he wasn't living right. He prayed, "'O Lord, I've broken most of the commandments. I've got some pretty bad habits -- I drink a lot, I curse most of the time, I steal things from work, I treat people like dirt. But, if my life is spared now I promise you that I will change, that I will never again curse, that I will never again steal, that I . . .' Suddenly his friend cried out to him: 'Wait a second, Jack. Don't go too far. I think I see another ship.'"

Solomon, in Ecclesiastics 5 says, "It is sinful to make rash promises to God... So when you talk to God and vow to him that you will do something, don't delay in doing it.... It is far better not to say you'll do something than to say you will and then not do it" (Ecclesiastics 5:2,4,6 LB).

#9 - GREEDS OR NEEDS

Do you ever have difficulty distinguishing between what are your needs and what are your greeds? Or what are true necessities and what you would like? The Bible says, God will meet all our needs... not all our "greeds" (Philippians 4:19).

On an episode of the television show St. Elsewhere, a grandmother and grandson were enjoying the sunny day as they strolled along the beach of the ocean. Suddenly a huge wave broke onto the shore and swept the little boy out to sea and out of sight. The grandmother was horrified. She fervently prayed, asking God to restore the child. A short time later the boy miraculously reappeared on the shore unharmed. Most of us would think the great need had been met - the prayer had been answered. But not for the grandmother in our story. After warmly embracing her returned grandson she said, "You know, Lord...he had a hat."

We say, "no way - that couldn't happen." No one would be that thoughtless and greedy. But it does happen when we fail to distinguish between our needs and our greeds. We often miss out on the blessings God gives us because we are disappointed that we didn't get more. We want so much but God gives us what we truly need.

#10 - SCULPTURING A CHILD

There is a sculptured head of Abraham Lincoln in the Capital in Washington done by Gutzon Borglum.   He cut it from a large square block of stone in his studio. One day, when the work on the face was about half completed, a young girl visited his studio. She seemed to have a strange fascination with the unfinished work. After staring at the piece for some time, she ran to the sculptor and asked, "Is that Abraham Lincoln?" "Yes", replied the artist.   The little girl said, "Well, how in the world did you know that he was in that block of stone?"

"Sons are a heritage from the LORD, children a reward from him," the bible reminds us (Psalms 127:3). In a sense, every parent has been asked to be a sculptor. They have been provided with a small child that has great potential, but which needs to be carefully crafted. Somehow the little girl seemed to think that Lincoln's face was already in the stone and all that the sculptor needed to do was break away the shell. We know of course that great skill was needed to chisel in just the right places. Our children also need far more than rudimentary breaking away of a shell. They need great help and attention if they are to be the masterpieces God intended them to be. One of our children dedication ceremonies says, "There is no gift more precious, more laden with blessing, more enriching to the home and family life, than the coming of a little child. However, with this great experience there comes also great responsibility to the parents for into their care is entrusted an immortal soul whose destiny is to a large extent determined by the character and influence of the home."

Parents, God has promised to help you as you as you chisel and shape the young life of your child.

#11 - COMMUNICATING CLEARLY

Communication is absolutely critical for good human relationships. A friend of mine often says, "faulty communication is what damns up the stream of life."

"Two inexperienced hunters went into the woods to hunt. The game warden was concerned about them getting lost so he instructed them that the signal for distress is to fire three shots in rapid succession.   Sure enough they got lost. One of them said to the other, 'You had better fire three shots?' So he did. Nothing happened. After waiting for about an hour or two, the first hunter said, 'You had better fire another three shots?' So the second hunter fired a second round of three shots. They waited another hour or so, and still nothing happened. Again, the first hunter turned to the second and said, in great distress, 'I guess you had better fire three more shots?' His friend said, 'I can't. I've run out of arrows?'*

How easy it is to think we are sending out the right signals when we are sending out silent arrows. We think the messages are clear, but no one else understands them. Couples often assume their mate should no why they are upset, when in fact the message is not clear at all. It is a guessing game. How much better to build a relationship where we can clearly communicate what we are feeling or desiring. Why not try saying, "honey, I wish you would .... or Honey, you hurt me when you said ..... Or still "honey, it meant a lot to me when you ...." Clear and precise communication is vitally important.

#12 - ENCOURAGEMENT

A friend of mine shared with me the following: "I was a 140 pound running back in high school. The guard on the line in front of me was 6 foot 4 and weighed about 230 pounds. On one play he provided down field interference for me. In the huddle after the play I criticized him for moving too slowly and impeding my progress. When I think back on that scene, I can still see icy brown eyes staring out from a dirt and sweat streaked face. On the next series the quarterback called a slant play over this same guard's position. He was supposed to shout post or flag indicating the direction he would block, either left or right. The linemen were in the set position. The center hiked the ball. The quarterback stuck the ball in my stomach and before I could take another step a defensive lineman crushed me to the ground. I lay there awhile waiting for the stars to fade from my vision and the air to return to my lungs. This time when we rehuddled I offered no criticism. The snickers and smiles of my team mates clearly spoke of where their sympathy lies. While I was faster and more agile than the guard, without his bulk blocking for me I was going nowhere."

Do you have someone who is helping you and who needs encouragement for what they do? You may be like the back that depends upon the guard to provide security and protection. If so, encourage this one who struggles on your behalf. Give them the recognition they desire and the help they require to make the victory certain. It takes no special ability to criticize.

It takes great courage to return to the battle whether it's play-after-play for football yardage or day-after-day for modest pay for a less than desirable job. You may be a spouse or single parent who receives little encouragement for what you do. You feel like you are playing the guard position for a family which could show you more appreciation? Take strength from Christ who is willing to take His place beside you. He has said, "Never will I leave you; never will I forsake you" (Hebrews 13:5).

#13 - CHOSEN AT LAST

Alice detested being paraded in front of the people who came to the orphanage looking for serving girls to work in their lavish homes. There were the stares and the searching eyes. There was the hesitation of the couples as they listened to her stuttering speech and saw the bad limp caused by a deformed foot. The feelings of being rejected were terrible.

One particular occasion didn't start out much differently than the others. Again, there was the muffled talk with the superintendent of the orphanage, the questions from the couple and Alice's stuttering responses. There was the bad limp that was usually the clincher for rejection. But, this time things were different. This time the couple said they wanted Alice. She stammered out her disbelief that they would want her to be their serving girl. The couple responded, "No Alice, we want you to be our daughter."

Alice could not believe what she heard. No one had ever said that to her before. "But, why me" Alice asked, remembering the many times she was turned down before by the others. The lady stood up and smiled at Alice. Slowly she reached down and lifted her floor length skirt and revealed her own deformed foot. Softly and lovingly she said to Alice, "Today we want you to be our child. Please Alice, let us love you."

The Bible reminds us that because of God great love, He invites us to be one of His children. He identifies with us in our suffering and pain.

#14 - DO WE REALLY CARE?

"Ma'am, I'm sorry to disturb you, but I'm collecting money for an unfortunate family in the neighborhood. The husband is out of work, the kids are hungry, the utilities will soon be cut off, and worse, they're going to be kicked out of their apartment if they don't pay the rent by this afternoon," said the distraught and despondent looking man at the door.

The Lady responded by saying she would be delighted to help. However, she had just one question. "But who are you?" she asked the man at the door. "I'm the landlord," he replied.

Jesus was talking about the final judgment and indicated there would be those who would pretend to be His disciples but were not. "We did this and this and these other things in your name," they implied, but Jesus said, "Sorry, I never knew you." Their service lacked sincerity and genuine caring.

It is easy to appear concerned if we are directly affected. If our children are sick prayer becomes insistent or the doctor's visit is imperative. However, if our issues are not directly challenged we may only go through the motions of concern. Pseudo concern is better than no concern at all, but it still falls short of genuine caring. The shortest path to your own happiness is the round-about way of making others happy first.

#15 - VOWS MADE - VOWS KEPT

Seminar leader, businessman and author Fred Smith writes,

"One of my treasured memories comes from a doughnut shop in Grand Saline, Texas. There was a young farm couple sitting at the table next to mine. He was wearing overalls and she a gingham dress. After finishing their doughnuts, he got up to pay the bill, and I noticed she didn't get up to follow him.

But then he came back and stood in front of her. She put her arms around his neck, and he lifted her up, revealing that she was wearing a full-body brace. He lifted her out of her chair and backed out the front door to the pick-up truck, with her hanging from his neck.

As he gently put her into the truck, everyone in the shop watched. No one said anything until a waitress remarked, almost reverently, 'He took his vows seriously."

I know several couples like this and it is beautiful. They have remained deeply committed to each other in spite of severe difficulties. They are models of love and fidelity.

It is encouraging to see commitment to marriage vows being taken more seriously. There are hopeful signs that marriage breakups are beginning to decline after years of steady increase. We are seeing a renewed awareness of the importance of the family unit. The Bible says that a husband "Must love his wife as he loves himself, and the wife must respect her husband" (Ephesians 5:33). As we put this into practice, our commitments can be maintained.

#16 - ANGELS

The Bible reminds us that angels are sent to help God's children (Hebrews 1:14). But are angels at work today? Greg Allen's missionary newsletter told a story that seems to indicate that angels are still active in behalf of God's people.

Greg described one of the most intense moments of his life. He had just twenty minutes to get his baggage on the overcrowded train out of Moscow. With bags falling and people cursing he began to load. In the midst of all this madness, the baggage handler began to shout and curse at him. He took Greg's papers, looked at them and told the workers to throw his luggage off the train. Why? What had Greg done?

In ten minutes the train would leave, so Greg prayed. It was not lengthy, but it was a sincere prayer. He simply breathed, "GOD, I NEED YOUR HELP." As he finished his prayer he saw his last bag being thrown out of the baggage car and one bag was seven feet down under the train on the tracks. Just then a man grabbed his coat, flashed a badge in his face and started taking him out of the station. The two men walked to a building with over thirty people standing in a long line. The man banged on the window and told them Greg was to be next. Everyone in line and in the office yelled at them to wait their turn. The badge came out again. He showed it to the crowd and then to the people in the office. In less than three minutes all of Greg's luggage was put back on the train. As for the man who originally ordered Greg's things off the train, he shook Greg's hand and said he would help him unload his things at his destination.

My friend, God still cares about His children and sends His helpers to minister to them and for them.

#17 - IN MEMORY OF MY BROTHER

Two memorial stones and two pine trees are located by the edge of the sidewalk just outside my home church in Ohio. These two markers are in memory of two young men from that church who gave themselves in service to their country: One is for a school boy friend of mine and the other is for my brother. I wish these stones were in honor of these two men rather than in memory of them. However, we can't turn back the clock on our lives and relive our school boy days, but such memories can cause us to be more thankful for those we may see everyday but take for granted.

The following illustration reminds us that we often fail to appreciate the daily gift of those around us and sacrifices they made. Parents of a young man who was killed in the World War gave their church a generous gift as a memorial to their loved one. When the presentation was made, another war mother whispered to her husband, "Let us give the same for our boy." The father said, "Why, what are you talking about? Our boy didn't lose his life." The mother said, "That's just the point. Let us give it because he didn't."

The freedoms we enjoy and privileges we take for granted were secured for us at a high cost by both the dead and the living. Why not stop a few minutes today and in some way express thanks for the sacrifices of so many on our behalf.

The Bible says " always giving thanks to God the Father for everything" (Ephesians 5:20).

#18 - DIVINE GUIDANCE

"All the way my Savior leads me what have I to ask beside, can I doubt His tender mercy who through life has been my guide." I have known of this hymn for years, but it came to have deep meaning for me as I stood and talked to an 80 year old husband and wife in a very small living room apartment in Beijing, China. These Chinese Christians had spent over 19 years in prison because of their faith. When we asked the wife what had helped her during those long and difficult years, her face became radiant and she began to sing this beloved hymn.

This hymn was originally written as an expression of gratitude to God after a direct answer to prayer. It is reported that one day the blind hymn writer, Fanny Crosby, desperately needed five dollars and did not know where she could obtain that amount. As was her custom, she began to pray about the matter. Within a few minutes a stranger appeared at her door with just the right amount. "I have no way of accounting for this," she wrote, "except to believe that God, in answer to my prayer, put it into the heart of this good man to bring the money. My first thought was, it is so wonderful the way the Lord leads me. I immediately wrote the hymn."

We too, can know that this same God who answered a blind song writer's prayer is willing and waiting to be our guide. But we must first ask Him to do this and let Him know that we want Him to be continually present with us.

#19 - HUMILTY

January 30, 1994, Thurman Thomas sat on the bench of the Buffalo Bills with his hands covering his face. The Bills had just lost the Super Bowl for the fourth straight time and Thomas' three fumbles had not helped their cause.

Sensing someone standing near him, Thomas looked up to see Emmitt Smith, star running back for the Dallas Cowboys, standing in front of him. What would the man who had just been named the super bowl's most valuable player be doing on the loser's side of the field? But there he was holding his goddaughter in his arms. As they looked at the dejected Thomas, Smith said to the little girl, "I want you to meet the greatest running back in the NFL, Mr. Thurman Thomas." This was not a put down or an attempt to rub salt into an open wound. Here was the concern for a fellow human being and a gesture of humility.

The Bible describes humility as a virtue. In several places the Apostle Paul says to "honor one another above yourselves" (Romans 12:10) and also "in humility to consider others better than yourselves." (Philippians 2:3). That sounds almost unthinkable in today's "dog eat dog" society. It sounds strange doesn't it? We hear so much about how to rise to the top, humility has almost been dropped from our vocabulary. The Bible is so bold at another point to suggest that we are not to be proud, "but be willing to associate with people of low position" and not to be conceited. (Romans 12:16). And Jesus reminds us that "the meek shall inherit the earth" (Matthew 5:5).

#20 - BOASTING

A Georgian farmer was showing a Texas farmer how big his farm was. "Our property line starts here," the Georgian said, "goes through those trees in the distance, along the stream on the left, across those hills way over yonder, back along that road on the right and back to this tree stump."

"Well," the Texan said, "that's pretty big. But back home on our farm, we get in the truck at sunrise and start to drive around the perimeter. Except for lunch and supper we have to drive until midnight to get completely around our farm.   What do you think of that?

"Yep," the Georgian replied, "I used to have a truck like that, too!"

We love to boast about what we have or who we think we are. People are constantly comparing their things with others to see who is on top. We love to think we come out first. But the Bible warns against boasting. Boasting assumes that we were able to provide whatever it is that we have by our own power, ingenuity and strength. The Apostle Paul says, "What are you so puffed up about? What do you have that God hasn't given you? And if all you have is from God, why act as though you are so great, and as though you have accomplished something on your own" (I Corinthians 4:7 LB)?

Jeremiah, known as the weeping prophet, said, "Let him who boasts, boasts in the fact that he knows the loving and righteousness God." (Jeremiah 9:24)

#21 - GOD NEVER CHANGES

When the Japanese invaded China many years ago, many Chinese as well as missionaries fled for their lives. One such missionary was Gladys Alward. But, how could she flee and leave 100 orphans behind? She couldn't. She decided to take them with her over the mountains to a free China.

The book, **Hidden Price of Greatness** describes what happened. During Gladys' harrowing journey out of war torn Yangching, she grappled with despair as never before. After passing a sleepless night, she faced the morning with no hope of reaching safety. A 13 year old girl in the group reminded her of their much loved story of Moses and the Israelites crossing the Red Sea. "But, I am not Moses," Gladys cried in desperation. "Of course you aren't," the girl said, "but, Jehovah is still God."

The little girl understood that it was God who made the difference in both situations. It was not the greatness of either Moses or Gladys. She was able to grasp the significance of the Bible story and recognize that though several thousand years separated the two vents, God had not changed. He was still the all powerful God.

You may feel very inadequate for some of the circumstances you are facing right now. But it may not be a case of your ability, but His. The God of Moses is still the same God.

#22 - TESTING MAKES ME STRONGER

The opening part of Ephesians 3:16 says, "I pray that... he (God) may strengthen you with power...in your inner being."   One of my parishioners wrote me not long ago and related how God had helped to strengthen her faith through a difficult circumstance. She writes,

"Our youngest son became very ill with asthma. We didn't have enough money to take him to the doctor but he needed medical treatment. We had an old Volvo station wagon parked in the back weeds behind our home for two years. The animals and the little creatures had made a home inside. I was on my husband's back all the time to take it to the junk yard. But still it sat there. Well, the very same day we needed to take our son to the doctor, someone came walking down our alley and asked us about the car. They offered us $50.00. We took the offer and thanked God because we now had the money to cover the doctor's visit and medication."

Part of our prayer for inner strength may be answered through various trials and tests. If things were always easy our spiritual muscles would become atrophied and weak. Just as an athlete works out to build up muscle and endurance so we as God's children are also tested in the competitions of life. The Bible writer James says, "Consider it pure joy, my brothers, whenever you face trials of many kinds, because you know that the testing of your faith develops perseverance. Perseverance must finish its work so that you may be mature and complete, not lacking anything" (James 1:2-4).

#23 - EMPATHY

Mr. Alter's fifth grade class at Lake Elementary School in Oceanside California had a group of boys like few classes have ever had. There were fourteen boys who had no hair. One of the boys had shaved his head rather than have his hair fall out in clumps because of chemotherapy for lymphoma. The other boys did the same so Ian O'Gorman wouldn't feel out of place.

In an Associated Press story (March 1994), 11 year old Scott Sebelius said, "If everybody has his head shaved, sometimes people don't know who's who. They don't know who has cancer, and who just shaved their head." They wanted Ian to feel like he fit in. When asked about what the actions of the boys meant to Ian, Ian's father choked back the tears as he said, "it's hard to put words to".

Is this not a little of what the Bible has in mind when it tells us to carry one another's burdens and in this way we will fulfill the law of Christ? (Galatians 6:2) The boys couldn't take the cancer or share the chemotherapy but they could make the road Ian was traveling a little less lonely and isolated. The boys wanted to identify with him in some way. They wanted to help carry his load.

There are people all around us who need someone to help carry their load. They are dejected to the point of despair and by coming along side them we can help to lighten their burden. By so doing we are identifying with Jesus, the greatest burden bearer of all time.

#24 - SPEECH LACED WITH GRACE

A man was discussing the secret of his rise in popularity. He attributed the new found success to just one particular word. "Years ago," he said, "upon hearing a statement with which I disagreed, I used to say "Baloney," and people began to avoid me like the plague. Now I substitute "Amazing" for "Baloney" and my phone keeps ringing and my list of friends continues to grow."

The Bible says, "A word aptly spoken is like apples of gold in settings of silver" (Proverbs 25:11). We can all visualize a beautiful silver bowl setting on an end table with golden apples filling the inside. Such is the beauty of thoughtful words spoken at the right time. The Psalmist said, "Let the words of my mouth...be acceptable in Thy sight, O Lord..." (Psalms 19:14).   Wherever possible our words need to be intended to enhance and beautify others. The Apostle Paul writes, "Let your conversation be always full of grace (unmerited love)...as you answer others." (Colossians 4:6).

We can all improve our speech toward others if we work at it. We may find we are received with a new response and surprising popularity if we just change a few little words like "baloney to amazing". Today, why not ask yourself if you like others to respond to you the way you do to them. If a change in your speech is needed, have the courage to do it.

#25 - DON'T QUIT

Someone asked James Corbett, the former heavyweight boxing champion, what it took to be a heavyweight champion, and he said, "Fight one more round!" When Thomas Edison was asked how he had been so successful in his inventions, he said, "I start where other men leave off?" The alma mater of Winston Churchill anticipated a great speech from him and were surprised when it contained only six words. The speech, though his shortest, was also one of his most famous. He simply said, "Never, never, never, never give up?" That was it; the speech was over.

Someone has written the following poem entitled "Don't Quit":

> When things go wrong as they
> sometimes will,
> When the road you're trudging seems all up
> hill,
> When the funds are low and the debts are
> high
> And you want to smile, but you have to sigh,
> When care is pressing you down a bit,
> Rest, if you must - but don't you quit.
> Life is strange with its twists and turns,
> As every one of us sometimes learns,
> And many a failure turns about
> When he might have won had he stuck it out;
> Don't give up though the pace seems slow -
> You may succeed with another blow.
> Success is failure turned inside out -
> The silver tint of the clouds of doubt
> And you never can tell how close you are,
> It may be near when it seems afar;

So stick to the fight when you're hardest hit -
It's when things seem worst that you must
not quit.

#26 - TATTOO ON THE MIND

Norman Vincent Peale in his book <u>Power of the Plus Factor</u> writes about walking through the twisted little streets of Kowloon in Hong Kong. He says, "I came upon a tattoo studio. In the window were displayed samples of the tattoos available. On the chest or arms you could have tattooed an anchor or flag or mermaid or whatever. But what struck me with force were three words that could be tattooed on one's flesh, Born to lose. I entered the shop in astonishment and, pointing to those words, asked the Chinese tattoo artist, 'Does anyone really have that terrible phrase, Born to lose, tattooed on his body?' He replied, 'Yes, sometimes.' 'But,' I said, 'I just can't believe that anyone in his right mind would do that.' The Chinese man simply tapped his forehead and said in broken English, 'Before tattoo on body, tattoo on mind.'"

The Apostle Paul knew the importance of the programming of the mind. He challenged his readers to think on things that were noble, right, pure, lovely, and admirable. He furthermore challenged them to continually dwell on things praiseworthy and excellent. These lofty thoughts and ideas lift us to the presence of God. They do not allow us to dwell in the mental gutter of despair and hopelessness.

How tragic for a person to think about himself as a born loser when God wants to make all of us winners through His power.

#27 - INVENTION

Around the turn of the century, young Clarence took his girlfriend for an outing and picnic lunch at a nearby lake. Clarence lovingly rowed in the hot sun, while his friend relaxed beneath the shade of her parasol. They finally reached their destination -- a small island in the center of the lake. After placing all their supplies beneath a shade tree, she sweetly reminded him that he had forgotten to bring the ice cream. Remembering his promise, he rowed back to the mainland. He found a small store, bought the ice cream, and made his way back across the lake. On his way up the hill to where his girl friend was sitting, she inquired whether he had remembered the chocolate syrup. Love is a strange motivator, so Clarence got back in the boat and rowed to the mainland once again. Half way back to the island Clarence stopped his rowing and spent most of the remaining afternoon dreaming about a faster and easier way to travel across the water. By the end of the afternoon the Evinrude outboard motor had been created in Clarence Evinrude's mind.

Are you like young Clarence, going through a time of testing or difficult circumstances? Rather than complaining ask yourself how you can turn those trial and adversities into stepping stones for success and growth. The Bible says, "Consider it pure joy, my brothers, whenever you face trials of many kinds, because you know that the testing of your faith develops perseverance.

Perseverance must finish its work so that you may be mature and complete, not lacking anything" (James 1:2-4).

#28 - PRIDE

Our high school senior class challenged all underclassmen o a tug-of-war. A huge tarp was covered with dirt and soaked with water to create a soupy mess. I took my place near the front of the line relishing the thought of dragging underclassmen through a muddy humiliation.

The signal was sounded and the rope strained from the force. Slowly and inexplicably we great and mighty seniors were dragged to an embarrassing defeat. I held fast to the rope even when all hope was lost. Pride did not permit me to do the sensible thing and release the rope and remain clean and unmuddied.

Pride is a force so strong it can cause us to do things we know to be stupid and harmful. Pride can cause us to deny what we know is true and to defend what we know in our hearts to be a lie. Pride can drag a person through the mud of sin and leave them wearing the emblem of defeat just as clearly as the mud from a tug-of-war.

Ironically, we may struggle most with pride around the people we love the most, our families. Pride tells us to rely more strongly on our own intuition rather than our spouse's counsel. Pride tells us to hide our mistakes from the children rather than have them think we are not quite with it.

The Proverbs says, "Pride comes before destruction and an haughty spirit before a fall." Daily we need to turn to Jesus asking Him to overrule our natural pride. We need to let go of the rope of pride that can drag us through the mud of sin.

#29 - ANGER

In his autobiography, "Number 1",Billy Martin told about hunting in Texas with Mickey Mantle on a friend's farm.   Mantle went to the house to get permission to hunt. The friend quickly granted the request but asked that Mickey would shoot a mule in the barn that was going blind and which he didn't have the heart to shoot.

When Mickey came out of the house, he pretended to be angry. When Billy asked him what was wrong, Mickey said his friend wouldn't let them hunt. "I'm so mad at that guy," Mantle said, "I'm going out to his barn and shoot one of his mules!"

Martin protested that he couldn't do that.

Mickey shouted back, "Just watch me."

When they got to the barn, Mantle took his rifle, ran inside, and shot the mule. As he was leaving, though, he heard two other shots. He saw that Martin had taken out his rifle also.

"What are you doing, Martin?" he yelled.

Martin with his face red with anger, said, "We'll show that guy! I just killed two of his cows!"

Anger can be dangerously contagious. The Proverb says, "Do not make friends with a hot-tempered man...or you may learn his ways" (Proverbs. 22:24-25). The Bible also says, "Do not be quickly provoked in your spirit, for anger resides in the lap of fools" (Ecclesiastes 7:9).

Most anger does not provide clear thinking. Counting to ten is indeed a good place to start.

#30 - SHOTDOWN

On September 1, 1983 Korean Air Lines Flight KE007 was shot down and all persons on board perished after the plane strayed into Soviet air space. Flying patrol for the USSR that fateful night was Major Osipovich. He usually flew during the day, but he wanted to give a speech on peace to a group of school children, so he changed shifts with another pilot.

Soon the Soviet pilot was caught in a series of blunders and misinformation. In the end, Major Osipovich followed orders and shot down the unidentified aircraft. The actions of an air force major preparing to talk about peace plunged 240 passengers to their deaths and sparked an international incident that pushed world powers to a stand-off.

Blunders and misinformation can also be damaging to people on the ground that we meet every day. Such errors may never cause an international incident like that of our story nor the deaths of hundreds of people, but they can badly hurt others and damage relationships. Every word of gossip and hearsay is based on possible misinformation. Transmitting that information to others is like sending out faulty data to the pilot. However, you and I have more latitude for action than the pilot. We can research the truth for ourselves if we think it necessary and we can make our own decision what to do with the information. We have the opportunity to spread the message of peace or to destroy others with the power of our tongue.

#31 - MAKING OURSELF LOOK GOOD

Joseph Stalin was short - just five feet, four inches tall. Furthermore, a childhood accident had let his left arm paralyzed and his hand slightly disfigured. Wanting to look good in a portrait, the artist was ordered to paint the picture as though looking up at Stalin. This made him look bigger than he was. Furthermore, Stalin folded his hands over his stomach making them appear firm and powerful.

It is human nature to put ourselves in the best possible light. But, we can take that too far and actually move into a life of falsehood and a fantasy world. Any personnel director will tell you that many resumes do not seem to match the people who submitted them. Surface appearances can be deceiving. In working with people you find that with some you get far less than they wanted you to think your were getting. While others never try to make a show of themselves and you end up getting far more than you thought you were getting. The Bible says, "Do not think of yourself more highly than you ought, but rather think of yourself with sober judgment, in accordance with the measure of faith God has given you" (Romans 12:3). We are to do our best to honestly evaluate ourselves - not over or under estimating who we are.

Honest self evaluation is not easy, but it is absolutely essential for good healthy living. An honest evaluation of our gifts, abilities, strengths and weaknesses is a first step to emotional wholeness.

#32 - ATTITUDE

Buckner Fanning tells the story of a pastor friend who developed a heart disease that left him tired and unable to function as a pastor. His doctors left him little hope of quality or quantity of life. In frustration he went to another state to inquire of a heart specialist who concentrated his work on the pastor's dilemma. After a long and rigorous examination, the pastor asked, "Can you help me?" The doctor who was not long on conversation said, "Yes!" After surgery was performed and recovery completed, the pastor returned to his church with a new lease on life. Several weeks later the pastor returned for a follow up examination. He thanked the doctor again and again for returning quantity and quality to his life. The doctor said, "I have had a part in helping you go on living, but the quality of life is now up to you."

All of us will face the storms of life and God has promised to be with His children in and through the storms, but the question that is ever before us is, "Will there be a quality in my life?" Will the trials of life make me bitter or better? Depressed or determined? Soured or strengthened? Perhaps the best question that can be asked is not why did this thing happen, but what can I become because of it? The Bible says, "And we know that in all things God works for the good of those who love him, who have been called according to his purpose" (Rom 8:28).

#33 - RENEWING OUR EMOTIONAL BATTERIES

Are you one of many in today's society who feels stressed out, tired most of the time, and with your nerves nearly to the breaking point? God's intent was that we would respond much better to life's stress than most of us do.

Michael Dickinson, from the University of Chicago, was quoted in the *Detroit News* as saying that "flies are the f-16s of insects, thanks to tiny elastic springs that turn their wings into efficient motors that recycle energy."

Dickinson's research, done inside a virtual reality flight simulator, discovered that insects require up to 100 times the energy consumption of an animal at rest. In comparison, an athlete running the 100 yard dash uses only about 15 times the energy of a person at rest. Dickinson reported in the journal Science: "Our findings suggest that insects in general must be using elastic storage as a means of minimizing energetic flight costs."

You may be saying, "Where can I get some of that "elastic storage" for my life? The Bible says, "... Those who hope in the Lord shall renew their strength" (Isaiah 40:31). Our renewed strength and energy comes from a daily dependency on God. We were not designed to get one charge at birth that would last our life time. Our storage batteries are recharged through daily times of renewal with God.

#34 - TRAIN A CHILD

It was a blistering hot day, the house was full of guests, and things weren't going too well. Finally, the hostess got everyone seated for dinner and asked her seven-year-old daughter to say grace. "But mother," said the little girl, "I don't know what to say." "Yes you do," said her mother, "just say the last prayer you heard me use." Obediently, the child bowed her head and recited hesitantly: "Oh, Lord, why did I invite these people on such a hot day?"

This humorous illustration reminds us of the importance of teaching our children correctly - not just teaching them.   "Sons are a heritage from the LORD, children a reward from Him," the Psalmist reminds us (Psalms 127:3).

If we see children as a reward or gift from God we will sense an accountability to Him for their training. In one of our Baby Dedication ceremonies we ask the parents of the children, "Do you recognize the serious responsibility which comes to you with the gift of this child and that is it your duty to teach and train him from his earliest years for the service of God as He instructed His servants of old? Do you recognize it is your duty and sacred trust to bring him up in the nurture and the admonition of the Lord?

All parents teach their children, it is just a matter of what they are teaching and how it is taught. God has entrusted all parents with a very special task for which we owe Him an accounting.

#35 - TRUST

A Canadian pastor, in a period of great despondency, received the help he needed from reading the following delightful true incident. The local parks commission had been ordered to remove the trees from a certain street which was to be widened. As they were about to begin the foreman and his men noticed a robin's nest in one of the trees and the mother robin sitting on the nest. The foreman ordered the men to leave the tree until later.

Returning, they found the nest occupied by little wide-mouthed robins. Again they left the tree. When they returned at a later date they found the nest empty. The family had grown and flown away. But something at the bottom of the nest caught the eye of one of the workmen - a soiled little white card. When he had separated it from the mud and sticks, he found that it was a small Sunday school card and on it the words, "We trust in the Lord our God".

We too often worry and fret about life's uncertainties. Such worrying robs us of much of the joy that we should be experiencing, while all the time God wants us to place our trust in Him.

Jesus shared an illustration about how the little birds are cared for by a loving heavenly Father and then He adds these words "are you not much more valuable than they?" (Matthew 6:26). The Bible further reminds us to "cast all our anxiety on Him because He cares for us" (I Peter 7:7).

#36 - FINDING POSSIBLITIES

How come some people seem to so good at being able to make lemonade out of lemon situations, while others know of nothing better to do than complain?

A truck driver who was hauling dirt for a landfill backed his truck up too and far put his rear wheels in a ditch. The weight of the load lifted his front wheels several feet off the ground. This was not a good situation. "What were they going to do now?" questioned the helper riding with him. The driver thought for a moment and then went and got some things out of the cab. He quickly slid himself under the truck and said, "I guess I'll grease her. I'll never have a better chance!"

What we do with life's perplexing situations often make us or break us. Do we see them as problems or possibilities? If we see them as possibilities then we will constantly be looking for good things. We will be looking for insights that can turn even a bad situation to our advantage. It can be like turning over an unexpected rock only to find a hidden treasure.

If we are in the frame of mind to look for possibilities then we will find them. However, if we only see the negative side of things then the opportunities will probably pass us by. The most beautiful gems in life are often found only after digging through the hardest rock.

#37 - ABILITIES

Do you feel you could have played the piano well if only you would have "practiced"? Have you ever found yourself telling your children they could be very good at something if only they would practice?

Fritz Kreisler, a magnificent violinist, never liked to practice. His wife, who was deeply concerned about his career, repeated kept after him to do it anyway. Mr. Kreisler seemed to work as hard at finding excuses not to practice as his wife did at trying to get him to practice. Toward the end of his life, a great banquet was held in Kreisler's honor and one speaker after another rose to speak of him in glowing terms. One even said, "He is the world's greatest living musician." Beaming, Fritz Kreisler turned to his wife and said, "Did you ever hear such praise?" Without cracking a smile, Mrs. Kreisler said, "Yes, but think what they could have said if you had practiced!"

Jesus told the story of three different people who were given various amounts of money to invest for their master. The first two servants doubled their principle but the third servant hid his money in the ground. When the master came back he was grateful for the wise stewardship of the first two but became visibly upset with the carelessness of the third. We all are given a certain number of abilities. It is what we do with them that is important. The ability we receive is God's gift to us but what we do with that ability is our gift to God.

#38 - SHALL NOT WANT

"I shall not want" is the second sentence of the 23rd Psalm. The Psalmist either had everything he could possibly dream of or else he had learned a great secret to contentedness. The word "want" can either mean every appetite has been satisfied or his basic needs had been supplied and therefore he was content.

Too often we think we must supply every craving that comes to our minds. You may have heard the saying, "The person with the most toys when he dies - wins." However, the person with the most toys when he dies - still dies. Experience has proven that people with the most toys don't necessarily win nor are they most contented. Sometimes they are extremely miserable.

The Shepherd gave the Psalmists enough of the right things to make life worth living. These things supplied him with purpose and meaning. He didn't lack anything. He had all he needed. The Psalmist in another place said, "Delight yourself in the LORD and he will give you the desires of your heart" (Psalms 37:4).

If your life is centered on trying to acquire everything you think you want, you will not find contentedness. Contentment is not found in things.   Rather, contentedness is found in a right relationship with your Creator and in giving your life away. Jesus said, "Whoever loses his life for my sake will find it" (Matthew10:39). With what the Shepherd provides, you too can say "I shall not want".

#39 - FOLLOWING ROAD SIGNS

Years ago, when a friend of mine had only been driving a short while, he traveled to Detroit. It was his first time driving in the big city. He turned a corner and found himself faced with three lanes of oncoming cars. That's right; he had turned the wrong way down a one way street. The only escape he saw was to drive up on the sidewalk around a parked car and back onto the street, this time with the flow of traffic. Obviously he could have avoided this frightening and embarrassing situation if he had been watching for all the signs and not just those identifying the streets.

The Bible is also full of signs. God Himself gave to Moses one particular set of signs which are called the Ten Commandments. In a manner of speaking, they are road signs for life. If everyone on earth would follow these road signs there would be no need for prisons. In fact, if no one would kill, steal or covet another's possessions this world would be paradise.

I have heard people reject the Ten Commandments as out of date and too narrowly confining.   But, the Ten Commandments, like road signs, provide the limits and direction I need to reach my destination in peace and safety. Make it your daily habit to read the Bible and to follow it's signs that lead to abundant life.

#40 - A LIGHTHOUSE

A lighthouse was being built on a remote island in the Pacific. The natives of the island watched with interest the construction of this new structure that dotted their landscape. They had never seen such a thing before and clearly did not understand what it was to do. Finally the big day arrived when construction was completed and the equipment was to be tested. As the fog slowly rolled in, they watched and listened with interest to the sight and sounds coming from the lighthouse. They lingered around for a little while and then slowly began to disband with apparent disappointment and sadness. One of the project engineers proudly asked a native what he thought of the operation. The native coldly replied, "The light shines, the bell rings, the horn blows, but the fog keeps on just the same."

Lighthouses were never designed to keep the fog away but to warn ships not to come too close to the rocky shore. Lighthouses are only helpful when warnings are observed and we stay away from that which would cause us deadly hurt.

Jesus said we are the light of the world. We are to be lighthouses that warn people to avoid dangerous areas that can cause disastrous results to their lives. We may not be able to keep all the fog away but we can be a beacon of warning to others.

John Wesley said, "He who governed the world before I was born shall take care of it like-wise when I am dead. My part is to improve the present moment."

#41 - GOOD EXAMPLES

The coach called the Little Leaguer in from center field for a conference. Eddie wasn't sure what he had done nor what to expect when he got to the dugout. The coach was in a very serious mood. When he arrived at the bench the coach said, "Eddie, you know the principles of good sportsmanship that the Little League practices. You know we don't tolerate temper tantrums, shouting at the umpire, or abusive language. Do I make myself clear?"

Yes, sir," replied the Little Leaguer.

"Well, then Eddie," sighed the coach, "Would you please try to explain it to your mother?"

Jesus said in His Sermon on the Mount, "You are the light of the world. A city on a hill cannot be hidden.... Let your light shine before men, that they may see your good deeds and praise your Father in heaven" (Matthew 5:14-16).

Adults are to be good examples. A brother and sister were fighting and one of the parents told them to quit. The children informed the parent that they weren't fighting. They were just playing mom and dad.

We are to set a standard that children and youth can follow.   What children learn from us is more often caught than taught. Many of the great teaching moments are the times when we are simply being observed by our children. Someone has said, "Others will follow your footsteps quicker than your advice."

#42 - RENEWAL

I look forward every summer to several weeks of vacation at our friend's cabin at beautiful Higgins Lake, located in the northern portion of Michigan's Lower Peninsula. This is a wonderful location for renewing my physical and spiritual batteries. I need these times of refreshing in part because of my nature. I am a doer and feel that if things are going to happen it depends on me. I tend to carry more stress than I should and make life less restful than necessary. One summer I was particularly stressed. The load seemed extra heavy and you know what that can do to the spirit.

During that week of vacation I was reading from the Bible and a particular verse seemed to jump off the page just for me.

The passage was telling about a group of people who were facing formidable opposition from outside enemies. Their failed course of action was one of "rugged individualism," a "we can do it by ourselves" mentality. But God wanted them to come to Him for help. He wanted them to turn from their sin and let Him provide deliverance. God says to them through the prophet Isaiah, "In repentance and rest is your salvation, in quietness and trust is your strength..." (Isaiah 30:15).

As I read that verse I thought some of it surely fit me. My spirit had not been particularly quiet and I was not trusting as I should. Consequently my inner strength and energy was being sapped. As I began to rely less on myself and more on God I was wonderfully renewed.

#43 - KNOWING WHEN TO FLEE

A humorous article in the Danbury, Connecticut "News-Times" relates that a hospital administrator was startled to see a patient fleeing down the hall out of the operating room. He stopped the patient and said, "Do you mind telling me why you were running away from your surgery?" The patient looked at him with startled eyes and said, "It was because of what the nurse said." The administrator said, "Oh, what did she say?" "She said, 'Be brave! An appendectomy is quite simple." The administrator said, "It is quite simple. I would think that would comfort you." The patient said, "I'll tell you why I ran: the nurse was talking to the doctor - not me."

There are times to flee certain situations. The Apostle Paul, author of 13 of the books that make up the Bible, warned Timothy, a young understudy, to run from certain things. He was to evade things that were as ominous to him as the unskilled doctor was to the patient. Timothy was told to flee sexual immorality, idolatry and the love of money. Each of these things if not avoided would bring about the down fall of the young man. He was to run from them as quickly as he could, not stay and try to fight them. The best way to avoid most punches of the enemy is just not to be there when he swings.

#44 - CONTROLLED POWER

Power can be used in at least two ways: it can be unleashed, or it can be harnessed. The energy in ten gallons of gasoline, for instance, can be released explosively by dropping a lighted match into the can. Or it can be channeled through the engine of a small sized car in a controlled burn and transport a person 350 miles. Explosions are spectacular, but controlled burns have lasting effect: staying power.

The Holy Spirit works both ways. At Pentecost, he exploded on the scene; his presence was like "tongues of fire" (Acts 2:3). Thousands were affected by one burst of God's power. There were shock waves that went out from that explosive event the touched the then known world in a matter of weeks or months. But there had to be more than just one large explosive moment. What has followed has made the difference in the Christian church.

The Holy Spirit also works in a more controlled or subdued way through the individual believers that make up God's great church. He works in us for the long haul. It is the Holy Spirit that helps keep individuals on course down the road of life. He is that constant source of controlled power that helps weary believers traverse the mountainous highways of a hostile world or forge the wild streams of difficult circumstances. Usually it is not some spectacular event, but rather the hour by hour and day by day controlled burn of the Holy Spirit at work within us.

#45 - HONESTY IS THE BEST POLICY

A small boy was asked to testify in an important law suit. While on the witness stand, he was cross examined by the opposing attorney. The attorney, hoping to win a significant victory, asked the boy, "Your father has been telling you how to testify, hasn't he?" "Yes," the boy immediately replied. Thinking he could now destroy the boys damaging testimony the lawyer asked, now, just tell us how your father told you to testify." "Well, father told me the lawyers would try to tangle me in my testimony, but if I would just be careful to tell the truth, I could repeat the same thing every time."

Truthfulness is the bedrock of our society. It is the foundation stones for the super structure of our civilization. Industry, schools, government, the church and every other element of society is blessed when honesty is used as the only policy - not just the best policy when convenient.

When King Josiah directed the work on the temple to be done, he did not even ask for a report of how the funds were spent. It says. "they did not require an accounting...because they acted with complete honesty" (2Kings 12:15). Let's pray and work to that end in our own society.

#46 - THE SOURCE OF FAITH

One of my parishioners is battling fast growing cancer. It is robbing her of much of her vigor and strength. I fervently pray before I visit that I may impart some word of hope and faith to her.   But faith comes hard when you see the affects of cancer and the corresponding treatments. However, it is at times like this when faith truly begins to work. My parishioner is a constant inspiration of faith.

We can't say how much faith we have when all is going well. Just like we don't know how strong we are until we are tested in competition. When my brother was killed in a plane crash, my father said, "This is when our faith really goes to work." Jesus often said to people in life threatening situations, "Have faith in me." They were asked to truly believe when it was most difficult and at their time of greatest need. And their faith was rewarded.

Faith asks us to look beyond our disease, fears, loss of job, sick children or any number of other obstacles to the one who is the true source of our help. Our problems say to us that the door is closed while God says He has provided a window. Today you may be struggling with something that seems relatively simple or with something as great as a terminal disease. The Bible asks you to put your faith in the One who is the source of all hope and power.

#47 - BECOMING A NEW CREATION

London businessman Lindsay Clegg told the story of a warehouse property he was selling. The building had been empty for months and needed repairs. Vandals had damaged the doors, smashed the windows, and strewn trash around the interior. As he showed a prospective buyer the property, Clegg took pains to say that he would replace the broken windows, bring in a crew to correct any structural damage, and clean out the garbage. "Forget about the repairs," the buyer said. "When I buy this place, I'm going to build something completely different. I don't want the building; I want the site."

Our plans for self-improvement are pale when compared with what God has planned for our lives. We often bring to him the broken pieces of an empty life and offer to repair and replace them. We may have very good intentions and truly strive to be better. But still we seem to come up short.

God wants us to have life and have it abundant and full. He reminds us that he doesn't want our feeble efforts of self reform but He wants the property so He can build something of His own choosing - something that will have eternal value. Self-reform may have some benefits but letting God completely remake us is by far the best.

The Bible says, "If anyone is in Christ, he is a new creation; the old has gone, the new has come" (II Corinthians 5:17).

#48 - THANKFUL

Do you ever get depressed thinking that nothing, or at least not much good ever happens to you? That you don't have many things to be thankful for?

Charles Krieg tells about Henry who was looking glum and depressed. A friend asked Henry, "What's the matter with you? You look like you've lost your last friend." Henry responded, "What's the matter? I'll tell you. Remember two weeks ago, my Aunt Molly died and left me $50,000?" His friend said, "Yes, I remember. What's so awful?" "What's so awful you ask? Remember last week my Uncle David died and left me $100,000?" His friend said he remembered that too and asked, "What's so bad about that?" With a sad face Henry responded, "What's bad about it? This week, I inherited nothing."

We would prefer to live with an unceasing flow of God's perceived blessings but that doesn't always happen. There are times that the blessings from God seem to come to us in waves - like water rushing over Niagara Falls. While at other times it seems as a mere trickle of blessing like that of a small stream during an arid summer.

It's important to remember during the dry times that God has been extremely faithful and good to us in the past. He never changes. What makes the difference is our attitude to His blessings. Rather than complaining because we didn't get more we need to be thankful for what we did receive.

#49 - INNER STRENGTH

The Queen Mary was the largest ship to cross the oceans when she was launched in 1936. She served faithfully through four decades and a world War. At the end of her active service she was anchored in Long Beach, California and became a floating hotel and museum. During the conversion, her three massive smoke-stacks were taken off to be scraped down and repainted. But on the dock they crumbled. Little was left of the 3/4-inch steel plate from which the stacks had been formed. About all that remained were more than thirty coats of paint that had been applied over the years. The steel had rusted away.

Sometimes outward appearance covers up what's on the inside. We call it hypocrisy - appearing to be something we aren't. Jesus called some people of His day, "whitewashed tombs". They put on a great show on the outside but inwardly were dead and empty. Deceit, fear, inferiority, jealousy and many other problems are daily covered up in attempt to appear bigger and better than is really the case.

The apostle Paul knew the possibility of inward collapse and the potential to try and cover it up. Therefore, he prayed specifically for his friends that they would be strengthened in the inner person. They needed reinforcement. He didn't want people to go through life with just a thin layer of veneer holding them together. He wanted them to be true through and through.

#50 - DO WHAT YOU CAN

In Elmer Bendiner's book, "The Fall of Fortresses", he describes one bombing run over a German city: Their B-17 was barraged by flack from Nazi antiaircraft guns. Their gas tank was pierced with a twenty-millimeter shell without touching off an explosion. The morning following the raid the pilot asked our crew chief for the shell as a souvenir of unbelievable luck. The crew chief responded that not just one shell had pierced the tank but eleven. Eleven unexploded shells when one would have blown them out of the sky.

The shells were sent to the armorers to be defused but to their surprise no explosive charges were discovered. These shells were blanks except for a lone piece of paper in one of them. The note on the paper said, "This is all we can do for you now." Tucked away in an occupied land was a munitions factory manned by people who wanted to help the allied cause in some way. It seemed small and rather insignificant but their brave action spared the lives of who knows how many men.

You may feel isolated, insignificant, overlooked and useless but you can do something. The people in our story could have thrown their hands up in despair and done nothing. But they did what they could. Whatever your situation, do something toward reaching the goal even if it is only small. Remember, *little is much if God is in it.*

#51 – DON'T FORGET ALL OF THEM

When Mr. Moody was once reading Psalms 103 and came to the verse, "Praise the LORD, O my soul, and forget not all his benefits-- , he paused and said, "You can't remember `em all, of course, but don't forget `em all. Remember some of `em." This seems easier for some than for others. You no doubt have friends who are always expressing thanks to God and other people and some of your friends don't have it so good from a human point of view. Yet they seem to be full of praise. Don't you just love to be around them!

On the other hand have you ever considered how you come across to others: are you a "thanker"? Do you encourage your friends by your expressions of gratitude? Are you a person with a grateful heart? May I suggest you do two things this week:

1. Listen to your own speech and note the expressions of thankfulness or lack of them. Are you a "thanker" or do you grumble and complain about your situation and circumstances? Sometimes we don't know which kind of person we are until we take time to listen. You might even get brave enough to ask your best friend to tell you truthfully how you sound to them.

2. Daily take a few minutes and list some of your blessings. This is not as hard as it seems. For example, when you are tempted to complain about not having enough money for a particular bill, try remembering how God supplied the money for all the other bills you were able to pay. Or, your health may not be the best, but why not thank God for your ability to see to read this book? The old church hymn had some good advice when it said:

"When upon life's billows you are tempest tossed, when you are discouraged, thinking all is lost, Count your

**many blessings, name them one by one, and it will
surprise you what the Lord has done."**

We can't remember all God's blessings, but let's be sure that we remember some of them.

#52 - MY NAME IS ON THE LINE

Have you ever heard anyone say "I have to do a good job because my name is on the line." Or, maybe you have heard someone else say "we will honor our product because our reputation is at stake."

Did you realize God promises to lead you in paths of right living because His reputation is at stake? According to Psalms 23 the Good Shepherd, "leads us in paths of righteousness for His name sake." He not only leads us because He loves us, but also to protect His holy name.

A young soldier was taken before Alexander the Great for disciplinary action. When the young soldier was asked his name he responded with "Alexander!" He again was asked his name and again responded crisply "Alexander, Sir!" Alexander the Great replied rather gruffly, "Soldier, either change your conduct or change your name".

God has a lot at stake in you and me. He created us and wants us to succeed in spiritual living. When we call ourselves Christians we need to be sure our conduct enhances His reputation.

#53 - NOT DESTITUTE

In his book <u>The Power of Positive Praying,</u> John Bisagno told of an elderly Russian woman who was being moved into low-income housing provided by the State. A friend asked if she had heard from her son who had immigrated to the United States. She excitedly responded that she had and that he had sent pictures of whom she thought must be his friends. When they walked into the woman's room they found her wall covered with five, ten and twenty dollar bills. The lady had been saving the pictures so her son could tell her about all his friends. The woman wasn't destitute. She had significant means but she just didn't know it. She hadn't called on the resources she had available.

The child of God also has an immense resource of help available that is ours for the asking. God said to the writer Jeremiah, "Call to me and I will answer you and tell you great and unsearchable things you do not know" (Jeremiah 33:3). The all wise God has ample provisions to meet all our needs, but He often waits for us to request His assistance. Our heavenly Father desires to help us as much as we desire to help our children. We don't force our assistance on them, but we are ready at a moment's notice when they call for help. Do you have some need today that could be met by using the 5's 10's and 20's you have hanging on your walls? The help is available just for the asking.

#54 - NO WOOL OVER THE EYES

The rod referred to in Psalms 23 was a short stick about the size of a policeman's night stick. One of its primary purposes was for protection for the shepherd and the flock. However, it was also used in other tasks of caring for the sheep. When the shepherd wanted to examine the sheep for wounds and disease, he would use the rod to help in parting the thick wool so he could get a better look. It helped him get beyond the surface appearance to the heart of the matter.

Our great Shepherd, the Lord Jesus Christ, also wants us to get past surface appearances and to the heart of the matter. He wants us to see what we are like at the center of our being.

God uses His Word, the Bible, as the rod to separate the wool and show us what we are. The Bible says, "For God's word is living and active...and is able to judge the thoughts and attitudes of the heart" (Hebrews 4:12). His Word penetrates deeply enough so the wool doesn't get pulled over our eyes.

The Psalmist said, "Search me, O God, and know my heart; test me and know my anxious thoughts. See if there is any offensive way in me, and lead me in the way everlasting" (Psalms 139:23-24).

#55 - MONUMENTS

How will you be remembered? How will your time on earth be marked after you are gone? How do you plan to perpetuate your memory?

Ahmed and Omar were two brothers from Arabia - each wanting to be remembered long after they were deceased. Omar chose to have an impressive looking stone monument of himself erected at a major crossroad on a well traveled caravan route. He had chiseled into the stone some of his alleged great accomplishments. The monument stood there for years - of no value to anyone.

Ahmed, on the other hand, chose a completely different way to be remembered. Alongside a very dry and dusty desert highway, he dug a well, planted date palm trees and made a shaded area for the weary and thirsty travelers. This area became a haven and rest for thousands. They blessed Ahmed's name and called him Ahmed the Good.

How precious and enduring is the memory of those who have lived for God and others. Their memories are not usually chiseled in monuments of stone or granite, but are erected in glowing and grateful hearts of those their lives have touched. The Bible says, "The memory of the righteous will be a blessing, but the name of the wicked will rot" (Proverbs 10:7). After monuments of stone and bronze have crumbled into dust, the deeds of love and kindness we have shown to others in the name of Christ will live on and on.

#56 - RICHES

A missionary on furlough was invited to dinner at a summer resort. Among the guests were many men and women of prominence and position. These people were dressed in the latest fashions and wore the finest in jewelry. They came to the meeting in the newest and best automobiles. The missionary, who had given his life and his wealth to bring the gospel to a needy people, was taken aback by all the wealth and opulence. He had visions how that wealth could be used to make life better for others. After dinner, the missionary wrote a letter to his wife: "Tonight," he said, "I had dinner at a wonderful hotel. The company was elite, but I saw strange things. There were some who wore one church, others wore forty small sound systems, and still others twenty libraries."

In our desire for "the good life" we often seek after material goals: a large home, a fast boat, a luxury car and the nicest clothes. We sometimes forget the needs of others. Jesus advises us, "Do not store up for yourself treasures on earth, where moth and rust destroy, and where thieves break in and steal. But store up for yourselves treasures in heaven, where moth and rust do not destroy, and where thieves do not break in and steal. For where your treasure is, there your heart will be also" (Matthew 6:19).

#57 - REVENGE

Retaliation is the desire or act of trying to get even for actions or words against us. Our revengeful spirit may be caused by unkind words spoken to us, losing the starting position on the team to someone else, or even worse. The Bible cautions us against seeking to get revenge - not only because it is contrary to the spirit of love, but often times it backfires on us.

A small boy was bitterly disappointed at not getting the part of Joseph in the school Nativity play. Rather, he was given the minor role of the innkeeper. Throughout the weeks of rehearsal he brooded on how he could get back at the one who got the part he wanted. On the day of the performance, Joseph and Mary made their entrance and knocked on the door of the inn. The innkeeper opened it a fraction and eyed them coldly. "Can you give us board and lodging for the night" pleaded Joseph, who then stood back awaiting the expected rebuff. But the innkeeper had not pondered all those weeks for nothing. He flung the door wide open with enthusiasm and obvious delight and cried, "Come in, come in. You shall have the best room in the hotel." The young Joseph was taken back for a moment. This was not part of the script. Then with an insight beyond his years and with great presence of mind, young Joseph said to Mary, "Hold on. I'll take a look inside first." He peered past the innkeeper, shook his head firmly and announced, "I'm not taking my wife into a place like that. Come on, Mary, we'll sleep in the stable

Our efforts for revenge can look as foolish and be as humiliating as that of the young innkeeper. The Bible says, "Do not repay evil with evil or insult with insult, but with blessing, because to this you were called so that you may inherit a blessing" (I Peter 3:9).

#58 - JUDGING

There is a poem by John Godfrey Sax some of us learned when we were children. It is called "The Blind Men and the Elephant", and tells how each of six blind men first "saw" an elephant. The first blind man happened to fall against the elephant's "sturdy side" and immediately decided that the elephant looked like a wall.

The second grasped the tusk and "saw" the elephant as a spear.

The third who felt the squirming trunk perceived that the elephant resembled a snake.

The fourth compared the elephant to a tree as he felt the elephant's knee.

The fifth saw the elephant as a fan because he felt the ear. And the sixth who felt the swinging tail saw the elephant as a rope. The poem concludes:

"And so these men of Indostan
Disputed loud and long
Each in his own opinion
Exceeding stiff and strong.
Though each was partly in the right
And all were in the wrong."

We too often are like the blind men: seeing only a small part of the elephant. We may be prone to pass judgments and jump to conclusions based on our blind observation of an elephant that we really haven't seen. Until we understand the whole picture, we cannot judge correctly.

Jesus reminds us, Matthew 7:1 "Do not judge, or you too will be judged."

#59 - THE REAL THING

A family was visiting a small town circus with their two young sons. The circus was hardly the "Greatest Show on Earth", and the hawkers were more talented than the performers. They peddled the foamiest (and stickiest) cotton candy, the brightest of helium-filled balloons, and the plumpest hot dogs.

One entrepreneur had a spiel that was attracting buyers. "Buy your genuine plastic monkey, here. It's a toy for every girl and boy."   The parents of the family of the two boys bought the smallest son a helium balloon, which the child clutched for a few seconds before it vanished into the blue sky. The older boy watched his "genuine plastic monkey" climb the wooden stick once before the salesman was out of sight. On the child's second try, the stick broke and the plastic monkey fell to the ground and fell apart.

Always after that when the children wanted some bright toy, the parents would remind the boys of the genuine plastic monkey. It became a family synonym for something shoddily made, but highly advertised.

However, there are still some truly genuine products and experiences; your faith can be one of those. In I Peter 1:7 we read "These (trials) have come so that your faith - of greater worth than gold, may be proved genuine and may result in praise, glory, and honor when Jesus Christ is revealed."

#60 - HIDDEN DANGERS

There is a modern picture by Stanley Berkley, entitled "The Hidden Danger" which deals with an interesting event at the Battle of Waterloo. It was this battle which decided the fate of Napoleon.

Throughout the day the battle had raged and things were not going very well for Napoleon and his troops. But neither had the great leader thrust his crack cavalry into the battle yet. These were the "Old Guard" who were always reserved for the times of greatest importance; these finest had never known defeat and anxiously awaited the command to enter the conflict. Finally the command came for them to charge. They appeared invincible. But there was one small problem - there was a dip in the road that neither they nor the famous General knew about. However, Wellington, the opposing General took advantage of it. He put some of his finest sharp shooters in the dip and they waited until Napoleon's cavalry were almost upon them and then they unleashed a decimating volley of shots. By the time the horses reached the dip their power was gone. Napoleon was defeated all because of a little dip in the road.

The little dips in the road of life may be the thing that does us in. The unexpected temptation, trial, set back or disappointment may send us reeling with little hope of recovery. That is why we need to constantly seek counsel from the wisest of counselors - the Lord Jesus Christ. He will help us to avoid the dips in the road that throw us off course or worse yet destroy us.

#61 - SUPPORT

Don Graham tells how one fall a young woman was traveling alone from Alberta to the Yukon. Linda didn't know you don't travel to Whitehorse alone in a rundown Honda Civic. The first evening she found a room in the mountains near a summit and asked for a 5 am wakeup call so she could get an early start. She couldn't understand why the clerk looked surprised at that request, but as she awoke to early morning fog shrouding the mountain tops, she understood. At breakfast two truckers asked Linda where she was headed. "Whitehorse." "In that little Civic? No way!" the truckers responded. "Well, I'm determined to try," was Linda's gutsy response. "Then I guess we're just going to have to hug you," the trucker suggested. Linda drew back. "There's no way I'm going to let you touch me!" "Not like that" the truckers chuckled. "We'll put one truck in front of you and one behind you and that way, we'll get you through the mountains."   So, all that foggy morning Linda followed the two red dots in front of her and had the reassurance of a big escort behind as they all made their way safely through the mountains.

There are people all around us that are traveling on dangerous and fog covered paths of life. Many of them just don't know how dangerous the road is they are traveling. That's where friends come in. They tell the person, "I guess we're just going to have to hug you." In essence we are saying that we are not going to let them travel down the dangerous road by themselves. We are going to be there with words of comfort and support.

#62 - OTHERS

"To live above with saints we love,
Lord, that will be grace and glory;
To live below with saints we know,
Well, that's another story."

Adam and Eve probably had difficulty getting along with one another especially after they ate themselves out of house and home. Cain, their eldest son, killed his brother and then had the nerve to ask, "Am I my brother's keeper?" We can tend to be very self-centered by nature: thinking only of our own needs and desires. A great many books have been written about how to get ahead by climbing over someone else to get there. But "getting it whatever the cost" is contrary to the teachings of Scripture.

The founder of the Salvation Army was not able on one occasion to attend the international convention because of illness. The conference was anxious to hear some word from their leader so he was encouraged to send a telegram. When the message arrived it contained only one word. Now, here was the leader of this international organization sending all the delegates just one word. But what a powerful word that became. The telegram simply said, "Others". That was the founders wish for the delegates.

Jesus reminds us that it is more blessed to give to others than to keep for ourselves.

#63 - SLANDER

The brother of Jesus reminded the early church they were not to "slander one another" (James 4:11). The Apostle Paul tells a young pastor that he is to "remind the people... they must not speak evil of anyone, nor quarrel, but to be gentle and truly courteous to all" (Living Bible).

It is alleged that a person had told all around a story of moral failure of another Christian. However, after a little simple investigation it was discovered that the story was not true at all. The tale bearer went to the person involved and apologized, but the damage was already done.

The offended person took a pillow of feathers and ripped it open. The feathers were then thrown into the wind. After this the slanderer was asked to collect the feathers and put them back into the pillow. The person however, protested that it was impossible. And so it was.

The object of the illustration of course was to demonstrate that just as it is impossible to gather all the feathers scattered to the winds so it is impossible to gather all the false stories that may be told. We indeed need to be careful when talking about others and to be "gentle and truly courteous to all." The Golden Rule is surely good advice when speaking about others.

#64 - BEATING BURNOUT

How to beat burnout is a popular subject today for writers, public speakers and corporate executives. But burnout doesn't just affect executives. Others, from assembly line workers to housewives also suffer from burnout.

But burnout isn't new - the Psalmist in Psalm 23 was delighted to know the Good Shepherd would restore his soul. He evidently at times felt spiritually burned out, empty, and with little feeling or enthusiasm. He knew the necessity of getting alone with God for rest and relaxation.

Life for you may be filled with too many commitments and too little time or too much work and too little strength. This fast pace may have left you numb and lifeless. You fulfill your responsibilities but your energy is spent. How can you change it?   Why not determine to set aside 15 minutes each day for the next two weeks for spiritual restoration. Read out of the Bible starting in either one of the Psalms in the Old Testament or from John in the New Testament or go through some of the great hymns from your church hymnal. You'll be surprised at the renewal you will receive from such a practice. Make spiritual restoration a top priority.

#65 - LOVE

A bus was taking a group of visitors on a sight-seeing tour through New York City. At one of the stops a little lad with tattered clothes, unkempt hair, and dirty hands and face stepped onto the bus. A woman asked the woman seated with her: "Where in the world is that boy's mother? Look at that dirt on him." The other woman responded, "Well, I'm sure that he has a mother, and I'm quite sure she loves him, but evidently she doesn't hate that dirt." Then she added: "I can tell you that you hate the dirt, but I don't believe you love the boy. Until loving the boy and hating the dirt can be combined, I'm afraid the boy will remain the same."

Too often we only see the "dirt" on others and fail to see their true value. We fail to truly love the person. Jesus said, what value is it if we only love those who love us? Even totally pagan people do that." The true test of our faith is to love those who don't love us.

Jesus was able to combine an intense personal love for others without justifying their sin. Jesus surely does hate the sins of the world, but at the same time He loved the heart of man enough and proved it to all mankind by shedding His blood on Calvary.

#66 - DRAINED

For some reason, I have never gotten into the habit of keeping my gas tanks on full. I don't know whether I don't like to take the time; I don't like to spend the money; or I think we will drive less if there is not much gas there; or if it is some kind of a game. My children will say to me, "Dad, you know we are on empty? And I usually respond, "No not really; as long as the needle moves we still have something in there."

The thing is to guess how far that something in there will take us. I missed several months ago coming back to town.

A car that runs out of gas in the wrong spot can affect many people or even endanger them. For example to run out of gas in a tunnel or on a bridge can affect and endanger 100's if not 1000's of others.

The same is also true of the person who is dried up - that has failed to take in the necessary emotional, physical, or spiritual nourishment. It might be a wife who regularly blows up at the children, the husband who verbally abuses his wife or the employee or employer who doesn't have the inner reserve to make it a pleasant day for others.

Without regular times of renewal we all can get to the point of running on empty. We are simply dried out. God knew that would happen so He gave us a commandment that says, "Remember the Sabbath day for worship and rest."

#67 - PRAYING HANDS

Gratitude for a friend's devotion became the basis for the famous painting of the "praying hands." Albrecht Durer had always wanted to be a painter. He left home at an early age to study with a famous artist. When he arrived at his destination there was another aspiring artist, who like himself, desired to study under a master. But how would they have income for living expenses? It was agreed that Durer would study and the friend would work at other employment to provide living expenses for both of them. When Durer's paintings began to sell then they would switch places.

Finally the day came when Durer's works began to sell. However, he soon discovered that his friend's hands had become crippled through the hard work that he had done. Durer was broken hearted over this turn of events. He was embarrassed that his friend had given so much for him.

One day Durer came home unexpectedly and saw the gnarled and twisted hands of his friend firmly clasped in prayer. As he observed the scene he said to himself, "I can show the world my appreciation by painting his hands as I see them now, folded, in prayer." Thus the touching story of gratitude and thanks became known through the world famous painting of the "praying hands."

Even more significant than the praying hands that inspired the famous painting are the praying hands of Jesus that were clasped in prayer for you and me many years ago. The beautiful prayer recorded in John 17 was not only for the disciples but also for all of us who would believe on Christ through their faithful witness. The Bible also reminds us that Jesus continues to intercede in our behalf at the right hand of God.

#68 - MONEY BELTS

Many years ago, it was common for rich people to wear "money belts" when traveling: similar to those seen today. Gold and silver coins were placed in pockets within the belt, which was then worn under a person's coat for safe-keeping.

In 1890, the passenger liner "Iguna" was crossing the Atlantic with 206 people on board. Many of the travelers were wealthy and were carrying money to Boston and New York. Late at night, the Iguna entered a thick fog bank; not able to see, the liner collided with a steamship, which hit the passenger ship broadside. The Iguna began sinking rapidly and many passengers were forced to leap into the water.

The crew of the other ship put out their life boats and saved 172 people in the water, but 34 men were lost. The crew of the lifeboats later explained that those who drowned were wearing money-belts, the heavy gold and silver dragged them under before they could be saved.

The parable that Jesus told of the Word of God that was sown on soil full of thorns and thistles represents those whose lives are too wrapped up in material things. Jesus says, "they hear God's Word but as they go about their work they are too concerned about life's worries, riches and pleasures and thus they never develop spiritually. Their desire for wealth literally chokes off the Godly influence. How tragic to be successful in man's eyes, as was the rich business man in the Bible, only to be called a fool by God. Make sure that which you save up outlives you.

#69 - GIVING PRAISE

Have you ever been embarrassed by the gratitude of others? Now some people are constantly looking for praise while others so much enjoy doing serving that they are truly flustered by the overflowing praise they receive for their service. Jesus reminds us that we should not go looking for praise when we are simply doing that which is our duty and responsibility. If praise comes it is nice but it should not be what motivates us to service.

The story is told of an Arabian oil sheik that made millions of dollars through the wise investment of a woman stockbroker. When the sheik offered to shower her with lavish gifts she refused stating that she was only doing her job. However, after steady insistence on the part of the sheik, the lady finally agreed "that a set of golf clubs would be a fine gift." One day, weeks later, a letter came from the sheik containing the following message, "So far I have bought you three golf clubs but I hope you will not be disappointed, because only two of them have swimming pools."

Not all of our service is recognized or praised in this life time. Much of what you do for others may go unnoticed or unappreciated, but Jesus reminds us that even a cup of cold water that is given in His name will not go unrewarded (Matthew 10:42).

#70 - OLDER BUT GROWING

Americans are living longer today. Life expectancy has risen ten years in the last fifty years and is expected to raise ten more in the next 50 years.

It is important to remember as we grow older that we never get too old to learn or serve. Grandma Moses was 76 when she started to paint. Cato at 80 began the study of Greek. Ronald Reagan was 69 when he began to serve as President of the United States and served until he was 77. Winston Churchill served Great Britain well at 77 during the war years.

The Old Testament promises were given to experienced men. Abraham was already old when God promised him his seed would be as the stars of the heavens or the grains of sand on the shore. His wife, Sarah was beyond the child-bearing years, but they had a son as God promised from whose line came Jesus.

Moses was 120 years old when he died. He had served his God while guiding the people of Israel in their wanderings and trials. Joseph died at 100 and Joshua at 110. The Bible respects old age.

Proverbs 16:31 states "Gray hair is a crown of splendor; it is attained by a righteous life."

Job asks, "Is not wisdom found among the aged? Does not long life bring understanding?" (Job 12:12).

God does not always promise good health for the aged, but He does promise strength. Deuteronomy 33:25 says "Your strength will be equal to your days." Isaiah 46:4 promises "Even to your old age and gray hairs I am he. I am he who will sustain you."

What better old age security do you seek than God's strength and sustenance?

#71 - WORRIERS

Some of us are chronic worriers. We worry that it might rain and ruin our planned outing...or that it might not rain and ruin the crops.

We worry that our children will move away and we will lose them...or that they will stay home and we will have to support them.

We worry that the doctor will find something wrong with us, so we stay away. But then we worry that if we don't go to him, we will feel worse.

We worry that prices will rise and the stock market will fall.

We worry that we might fail, so we do not try.

We worry that we might lose our jobs or become ill.

But worry is not the Christian way. Jesus tells us in His sermon on the mount, "Do not worry about your life, what you will eat or drink, or about your body, what you will ear. Look at the birds of the air; they do not sow or reap or store away in barns, and yet your heavenly Father feeds them. Are you not much more valuable than they? Who of you by worrying can add a single hour to his life?

We need to substitute faith for worry. Trust God's promise that says, "And we know that in all things God works for the good of those who love Him" (Romans 8:28). We also need to follow the Biblical advice we find in 1 Peter 5:6 where it says, "Cast all your anxiety on God, because He cares for you."

#72 - BALD EAGLE

The bald eagle was at the brink of extinction two decades ago. But it has made such a dramatic recovery that the Interior Department wants to remove it from the endangered species list. It marks a renaissance for the stately bald eagle - the nation's symbol for more than two centuries. The number of eagles has grown from 800 to 8000 during the last 20 years in the lower forty eight states.

The Bible says, "God satisfies our desires with good things so that our youth is renewed like the eagles" (Psalms 103:5).

How is this possible? How can we make dramatic comebacks like that of the eagle? For the eagle there is the molting process - when the old set of feathers are cast off and a new set begin to grow back. What the eagle does is to get on the rocks and let the sun bring the warmth and renewal to its frame.

And like the eagle, when we have become tired and weary, when the battle of life and the storms of temptation have knocked the stuff out of us, we also need to get to a place of renewal and molting. Rather than just the S-U-N we need to get alone with the S-O-N of Righteousness who comes with healing in His wings and let His love and warmth renew us.

#73 - AT MY DUTY

We often hear about the second coming of Christ. Periodically there are news accounts of a group of people who have gathered in one location to await this anticipated event which they believe will happen on a specific date. To this point the event has always passed with the group of disillusioned followers going back home to pick up the pieces of their lives. Jesus indeed stated He would return, but He did not specifically tell us when. He said we were to stay busy until He does come.

During John F. Kennedy's run for the presidency in 1960, he frequently concluded his speeches with the story of Colonel Davenport, the Speaker of the Connecticut House of Representatives. One day in 1789, the sky over Hartford, grew extremely dark. Some of the representatives peered out the windows at the threatening situation and concluded that the end was at hand. There was a growing chorus of people asking for adjournment. Davenport spoke to the members of the house and said, "The Day of Judgment is either approaching or it is not. If it is not, there is no cause for adjournment. If it is, I choose to be found doing my duty. Therefore, I wish that candles be brought."

We are not to fear the darkness, but rather we are to be beacons of light until Christ returns.

#74 - CUNNING

Major William Martin never knew the great contribution he made to the Allied success in the Second World War, especially in Sicily, because he died of pneumonia in the foggy dampness of England before he ever saw the battle front.

The Allies had invaded North Africa. The next logical step was Sicily. Knowing the Germans calculated this, the Allies determined to outfox them. One dark night, an Allied submarine came to the surface just off the coast of Spain and put Martin's body out to sea in a rubber raft with an oar. In his pocket were secret documents indicating the Allied forces would strike next in Greece and Sardinia. Major Martin's body washed ashore and Axis intelligence operatives soon found him, thinking he had crashed at sea. They passed the secret documents through Axis hands all the way to Hitler's headquarters; So while Allied forces moved toward Sicily, thousands and thousands of German troops moved on to Greece and Sardinia - where the battle wasn't.

Satan works with more cunning than even the Allied plan, getting us to move in directions we think are important but aren't. We end up giving first rate energy to third rate causes. The writer of the Proverbs gave the wise advice when he said, not to trust our own wisdom but to acknowledge God in all things and He would direct our paths (Proverbs 3:5-6).

#75 - TACKLE A LITTLE BEAR

The story is told of two men who were talking. One of them was huge, the other quite small. The small man was admiring the size of the larger man. "Boy, if I were as big as you are, I wouldn't be afraid of nothin'. I'd go out into the woods and find me the biggest bear and tear him limb from limb." The big fellow smiled. "There are lots of little bears in the woods. Why don't you go out and tackle one of them?"

How often do we limit ourselves because we think we are not gifted enough, don't have the necessary resources, don't feel we are as good as someone else, or don't think it is a big enough project? We make such comments as "If I was as gifted as so and so...," or "If I had their money then I would do such and such...," or "and the list goes on." To often we wait for just the right opportunity and we let pass all the ones that would have been just right for us and would have gotten us farther along the road than we would have dreamed. I was fretting one time about the slow progress of a building permit when a good friend reminded me that we still needed to "hustle while we waited". He was telling me there was still plenty of good work to do until the big project got started.

Jesus reminds us in the Bible that he who is faithful in the little things will be trusted with much bigger things. Perhaps most of us cannot take on the "big bear" of duty and responsibility, but this doesn't mean that we are to sit idly by and do nothing. Furthermore, it is going out and catching all the little bears which equips us to take on the bigger ones.

#76 - THE MORNING STAR

Several years ago I was going through a difficult time in my life. It seemed that things were going just the opposite way I wanted them to go. I remember praying and asking God if He knew what He was doing. I didn't think things were going like He would want them too either. Did He know what was going on? Was He really interested in the trends of things? Did He have things in control? It really got me down. I was discouraged over the issues.

Early one morning before the sun was up I was praying about this and telling God of my concerns. As I looked out the window I was able to clearly observe the morning star. The sky was crystal clear and that morning the star shone with wonderful brilliance. There came to my mind a thought that had not been there before, which I believe was the prompting of God. It was as though God said to me, "Bill, Do you see that star?" "Yes," I replied. "Was that star there yesterday?" "Why, yes, it has been there for thousands of years." "Bill, will that star be there tomorrow?" I had no recourse but to reply, "I'm confident it will be - that's a pretty sure thing." "And Bill, do you remember the verse of Scripture where Jesus said, "I am the bright morning star?" "Yes." "Don't you see Bill, I was here yesterday, am here today and I will be here tomorrow. You may not know what's going on, but I do. It's all under My control." This was not an audible voice that spoke to me, but the meaning was sure clear in my mind and was such a comfort.

And now several years later, I still often think of the morning star when passing through difficult times. Even when the clouds block my view, I am reminded that the morning star is still there.

#77 - WRONG DIRECTION

While driving on the turnpike late one dark evening, I missed my exit. The next exit was 27 miles away - that meant 54 miles round trip to get back to the missed exit - 54 miles of unnecessary driving and time. What choice did I have? Apparently None! Or did I? About 10 miles down the road, I came to one of those "emergency only" turn around places. What a moral dilemma. What should I do? Was this a emergency? Would my situation justify risking a run in with the law?   Have you ever faced a similar situation?

Sometimes life is like my driving experience. We miss our exit or get going in the wrong direction. We go miles out of our way and don't know how to get back. We make a mess of things before we finally figure out how to correct the situation.

Is that happening to you? Are you off course - going miles out of your way - getting into situations that you don't know how to get out of? STOP right now - correct your course. Turn around and head in the right direction...**GOD'S WAY.**

Thankfully we serve a God who encourages us to make use of those areas marked "Emergencies only". He wants us to make U turns.

#78 - MOTHERHOOD

Motherhood and home making is indeed a noble calling. No one should be ashamed of assuming a role of staying home and caring for the children when that is at all an option. And more often than not it is an option if we are willing to make it so. Too many times women are made to feel that they should apologize for being mothers and housewives. In reality, such roles are noble callings.

Joe Bray tells about when he was on the faculty of the University of Pennsylvania. His wife chose to stay at home and care for their children rather than find other work outside the home. There were gatherings from time to time to which faculty members brought their spouses. Inevitably, some woman lawyer or sociologist would confront his wife with the question, "And what is it that you do, my dear?" His wife had a great response: She said, "I am socializing two homo sapiens into the dominant values of the Judeo-Christian tradition in order that they might be instruments for the transformation of the social order into the teleologically prescribed utopia inherent in the eschaton?" When she followed that with, "And what is it that you do?" The other person's, "A lawyer" just wasn't that overpowering.

The intimate care for one's children is the highest calling of all. If God has blessed you with an opportunity to stay home and care for your children, thank Him. In the years to come it will no doubt be your most prized possession. And whatever you do - do it all to the glory of God.

#79 - FAITHFUL FRIEND

General Grant's faithful friend, his chief of staff, was John A. Rawlins. He was closer to Grant than any other during the war. It was to Rawlins that Grant gave his pledge that he would abstain from alcoholic beverages. When he broke that pledge Rawlins with pleaded with him, for the sake of himself, and for the sake of the nation, to refrain from strong drink. Faithful were the wounds of that friend.

In front of the Capitol at Washington today there stands the magnificent monument of General Grant, sitting on his horse in characteristic pose and flanked on either side by stirring battle scenes. But at the other end of Pennsylvania Avenue, a little to the south of the avenue, is Rawlins Park, where there stands a very ordinary, commonplace statue of Rawlins. And we can never forget this ordinary monument when we stand before the great monument of Grant on his horse at the front of the Capitol; for it was Grant's faithful friend Rawlins who kept the great general on his horse.

Today, why not take time to thank a special friend in your life who may be responsible for "keeping you on your horse."

#80 - ANSWERED PRAYER

Dr. Raymond Edman of Wheaton College had not been in Uruguay as a missionary very long when he became deathly sick. In fact, the Uruguay nationals had his grave dug, and were waiting close by to take his body away. Suddenly, Dr. Edman sat up in bed. He called to his wife, "Bring me my clothes. I'm getting up!" He had instantly recovered and nobody knew what had happened, or what had caused his recuperation. Many years later he was retelling the story of this remarkable recovery to a church in Boston. After the service, a little old lady with a small dog-eared, beaten-up old Prayer Book came up to him. She said, "What day did you say you were dying in Uruguay? What time would it have been in Boston?" They figured it would have been 2:00 A.M. on a specific date. Her wrinkled face lit up. Pointing to her book, she exclaimed, "There it is, you see? At 2:00 A. M. on that date, God said to me, 'Get up and pray -- the devil's trying to kill Raymond Edman in Uruguay!'"

God knows your need. He knows when to have someone pray for you or for you to pray for others. God did not just create the universe and then leave us. The bible says, "My God will meet all your needs according to his glorious riches in Christ Jesus" (Philippians 4:19).

#81 - PUTTING IN A GOOD WORD

A small Midwestern College was in the midst of an expansion drive. It was decided that various members of the faculty and staff would visit known benefactors and solicit contributions. As one particular professor prepared for his visit, he prayed that God would intervene and help his meeting be a success.

When he arrived at the businessman's office, he was greeted warmly by an young man that the professor recognized from one of his classes some years earlier. The professor couldn't remember the background of the young man, but he did remember how the young college student had sought him out for advice man at a crucial time in his life.

The professor shared the purpose of his visit with the young man before being taken into the father's office. As they entered the room, the young man said, "Dad, this is a friend of mine. He's all right. He's come in behalf of the college I attended." After a little discussion, the dad reached for his check book, inquired of the need and wrote out a generous contribution. The gift may have been made, but it was made much easier for the professor because of the good word of a friend.

Putting in a good word for others can be a valuable asset in helping them succeed in life. It can mean the difference between that all important break or puttering along with little more than an existence. You may be just the person to help.

The greatest example of putting in a "good word" is when Jesus does that for us in the presence of His heavenly Father. John the Apostle describes Jesus as the great Mediator who pleads before the throne of God in our behalf (I John 2:1).

#82 - CAUGHT

A penny pinching man was looking for a cheap gift for a friend. Wanting to look respectable and yet not spend more than absolutely necessary, he thought he had found the perfect gift. While browsing in a gift shop he saw a vase that had been broken which he figured he could buy for almost nothing. After the purchase, he asked the clerk to wrap the gift and send it to his friend. His logic was that his friend would assume that the gift was broken in shipping.

Several weeks went before the penny pincher received a thank you note. The note said, "Thank you for the vase. It was so thoughtful of you to wrap each piece separately." We are often reminded that we "can't full all the people all the time." But still people try. Story after story is woven and act after act is performed in order to make things appear what they are not.

Our attempts at half truths, cover-ups, and deceptions are usually discovered eventually. The penny pincher in our story had no idea the clerk would wrap the pieces individually before sending them. What seems hidden to the one trying to deceive is often quite visible to the on looker. The old saying, "Love is blind but the neighbors ain't" has confounded more than one marriage cheater. "Be sure your sins will find you out" is a law that has an amazing accuracy record.

#83 - IN PRESENCE OF ENEMIES

Is there someone you simply cannot stand? Do you feel they are crooked, unscrupulous and evil? You may have personally been wronged by them or have seen what they did to someone else. "It's not fair," frequently comes from your lips as you see this person continue to prosper and get ahead. You may even ask, "Where is God?"

The Psalmist was faced with a similar situation. He saw the wicked accumulating more personal possession, rising higher up the social ladder and seldom getting sick. While others who tried to do right seldom got ahead and often suffered physical illness. He questioned God. He began to wonder whether it was worth it to be good and do right. He came close to giving up a Godly lifestyle. Then he went to his church and he found out what the end of the wicked would be. He then began to feel sorry for those who left God out of their lives (Psalms 73:17).

A little girl who misbehaved was required to eat her meal at a distance from the rest of the family. The family did their best to ignore her so as to reinforce the punishment. All was going well until they heard the little girl praying. As they listened they heard, "I thank Thee, Lord, for preparing a table before me in the presence of mine enemies."

You may feel overwhelmed by what you see as injustices, but the closing words of the twenty third Psalms reminds us that God, somewhere down the road, prepares a table for us that will show us and our enemies that His way was right.

#84 - FINISH THE CANAL

Every leader will face a time of severe criticism. Their activities and motives may be brought into question. They may be considered out of touch, ideally minded, hair brained and any number of other choice epitaphs. How should the leader respond? Is it necessary to answer every criticism and negative comment, or is it good to wait awhile? Certainly circumstances dictate some responses, but Colonel George Goethals had a sensible response when severely criticized about his project.

Colonel Goethals was responsible for supervising the building of the Panama Canal. It was a monumental task when you consider the problems of climate, health for the workers and the difficult landscape to be channeled through. But Goethals believed the job could be done.

His critics in the United States were vociferous in their protest about this insane project. Not only did they question the more obvious issues confronting the project, but there was also strong opposition to the project itself. Why would we ever need such a canal? Who were the crazy people up in the front office that got us into this situation in the first place? There was more than one prediction that the job would never be completed. But Goethals worked on.

"Aren't you going to answer these critics?" an associate asked. "In time," Goethals replied. "How"queried the associate. "With the canal," was Goethals response.

Sometimes the best response is simply to finish the project the critics said would never get done.

#85 - FROST AND FRUIT

One of the dreaded enemies of fruit growers is frost. Many other things can be battled, but frost is so invasive and can cover so much area that a killing frost is hard to ward off.

The **Christian Worker's Magazine** tells the story of a young man who invested his life savings in developing an orchard of peaches. It was a risky investment, but if it was successful it would be worth it financially. One spring, when most of the blossoms were out, there was a late and hard frost. The crop was devastated and so was the young man.

The pastor noticed that the young man was not in church for two or three weeks and became concerned. He visited him at his farm. While they were standing at the edge of the ruined orchard crop, the pastor expressed his concern that the young man had not been in church. The young man somewhat angrily replied, "I'm not going to church anymore! Do you think I can worship a God who cares so little for me that He will let a frost kill all my peaches?" The minister replied, "God loves you better than He does your peaches. He knows that while peaches do better without frosts, it is impossible to grow the best men without frosts. God's objective is to grow men--not peaches."

God often allows difficult circumstances to come into our lives to build and shape us. We would prefer no "frost" touch our lives, but God knows we develop best when we have been touched by some frost. He is more concerned about growing us, than growing things we use.

#86 - THE GOOD SAMARITAN

On a personal trip to a third world country, I was riding in a car with a national driver. In one of the lanes of traffic was a truck on its side and burning. There was no one around and we could not see if anyone was trapped in the vehicle. My first inclination was to stop and see what assistance we could offer. However, the national from that country let it be known that we could not be the first ones to stop and offer help for fear of being mobbed by people thinking we caused the accident. I had other nationals warn me about stopping, but this was the first time I saw the practice at work.

I couldn't help but feel saddened by the incident. Was there anyone in the truck? Could we have made a difference? However, I was more troubled by the larger picture of seeming indifference to human need. Volunteerism and caring are so important to alleviating many of our social concerns, yet here is a country that is afraid to take that first step and reach out to needy people?

I was reminded of the Bible story of the Good Samaritan. There were two people who should have stopped to assist the beaten man, but didn't. A third person had every reason to pass on by, but chose to get heavily involved in helping. The last person was described by Jesus as the true friend.

I am thankful that "Good Samaritanism" is still applauded and in many ways protected. Let's continue to encourage and promote ready response to times of need and crisis.

#87 - A TRUTHFUL LIE

Have you ever known of a time when the truth was told, but it was told in such a way as to cast a shadow over someone's reputation? Facts were taken out of context in an attempt to hurt rather than inform?

The story is told of a young man who worked on a large ocean going vessel and tried hard to avoid many of the moral pit falls of youth. However, on one occasion, his carelessness led to his intoxication. The captain, who hated the young man, saw this as an opportunity to write him up and get him fired. He wrote in the log, "Mate drunk today." The young man pleaded with the captain to remove the entry and give him another chance since this was his very first offense. The captain refused stating, "It's a fact, and into the log it goes!"

A few days later, the young man was responsible for keeping the log and concluded his remarks with the words, "Captain is sober today." The captain quickly realized the implications if the wrong people should see this entry. He asked the mate to remove it from the log, but the mate responded, "It's a fact, and in the log it stays."

Even truth can be mishandled. People who would never want to be accused of telling an untruth can become skilled in twisting the truth. They can make it leave an impression that is not truthful at all.

The Psalmist describes righteous person as one who speaks the truth from the heart (Psalms 15:2). Truthfulness is as concerned with intent as with the words that are spoken.

#88 - WHAT IS SUCCESS?

In 1923 six of the most financially successful men in America gathered at the Edgewater Beach Hotel in Chicago. These six men had shown that they could make money and make a lot of it. The good life was now theirs to enjoy. They should have been set for life. But, were they truly successful? Where were these men 25 years later?

Charles Schwab, the president of the largest independent steel company, lived on borrowed money the last five years of his life and died penniless.

Richard Whitney, the president of the New York Stock Exchange, was incarcerated for a time in Sing Sing Prison.

Albert Fall, a former member of the President's Cabinet, was pardoned from prison so he could die at home.

Jesse Livermore, a financial wizard on Wall Street, Leon Fraser, the president of the Bank of International Settlement and Ivan Krueger, head of the world's greatest monopoly all committed suicide.

The media and many Americans idolized these men for their success at making money, but considering their outcome were they truly successful?

The Bible records an interesting statement that seems to describe what God considers success. It states, "Let not the wise man bask in his wisdom, nor the mighty man in his might, nor the rich man in his riches. Let them boast in this alone: that they truly know me, and understand that I am the Lord..." (Jeremiah 9:23-24). True success needs to be seen through God's eyes and not mans.

#89 - APPOINTMENT WITH DAD

A busy business executive was in the maternity waiting room in anticipation of the birth of his child. He nervously flipped through the pages of the year old magazines that cluttered the lamp tables. He then pulled a notebook full of papers out of his bulging brief case and began thumbing through them. He decided he might as well used this "down time" to catch up on some badly needed work. He was in deep concentration when the nurse stepped into the room and talked with him. "It's a boy, Sir," she said. "Well," snapped the executive without looking up from his work, "ask him what he wants."

Men tend to receive a significant amount of their self esteem from their job. A consequence is that they often devote long hours to their work which takes them away from their wife and children. Their employment engulfs them. It saps their time and energy. Young fathers are caught in the bind of trying to balance the building of a career at the same time they are trying to build a family.

It is important to early in life establish a core set of values in order to keep proper balance. What are the things that are most important to you? Forty years from now, what do you want have happened in your life? You will have time for all the truly important things, if you establish clear personal guidelines and then periodically check up on yourself.

#90 - DADDY'S DEN

One of the ways that men frequently mistreat their wives is by their speech. Often times this takes on a tone of harshness, sharpness, critical or hurtful comments. The husbands are simply not nice to be around. It reminds me of the story of the two little girls who were touring the new home of one of them. As they came to one particular room the little girl said, "And here's my daddy's den." She then proceeded to ask her friend, "Does your daddy have a den?" "No" her friend responded, "My daddy just growls all over the house."

No one likes to live with a grouch. It not only makes life miserable for everyone, it also destroys self-esteem. Its a happiness destroyer and sometimes a marriage wrecker.

The Bible teaches that husbands are to be kind to their wives and not harsh in their speech toward them (Colossians 3:20). The deeper meaning indicates that regular expressions of crossness are not to be a part of the Godly man's behavior. He is not to vent his anger and personal frustrations out on his wife. He is to treat her with respect.

Have you ever stopped to consider how your speech sounds to others? Has anyone suggested that you listen to yourself for a period of time? Would you like someone else talking to you the way you talk to your wife and children?

We can develop hurtful patterns of speech and maybe not even realize it. Why not spend time this week analyzing how you sound to others and make changes were necessary.

#91 - A CHEERFUL GIVER

Financial giving to religions organizations is deeply rooted in Scripture and is taught and encouraged in most churches. A six year old girl was sitting beside her father in a Sunday morning worship service. When it was time for the offering plate to be passed, the girl wanted to participate. The father agreed, thinking this would be one of those good teaching moments. He handed her a one dollar bill and also talked about how God loves a cheerful giver. As the usher handed the girl the offering plate, she looked at him with a rather blank stare. Finally she blurted out rather loudly, "Mister, don't you have change for a dollar?" The congregation could not hear what the embarrassed father said to his daughter, but it didn't take them long to figure it out. The little girl spoke up again and said, "But, Daddy, I'd be a more cheerful giver if I could give SOME to the Lord and buy a candy bar, too!"

The writer of the Proverbs reminds us that "One man gives freely, yet gains even more; another withholds unduly, but comes to poverty. He then summaries his thoughts on giving by saying, "A generous man will prosper; he who refreshes others will himself be refreshed (Proverbs 11:24,25).

God truly wants us to give with a joyful spirit (II Corinthians 9:7) and reminds us that as we give generously we will also reap generously (II Corinthians 9:6).

#92 - RECIPE FOR SUCCESS

An unknown author suggested a twelve month recipe for successful and happy living. Surprisingly, it does not focus a lot on the things that many think will bring them happiness. Also, it does not depend very much on good fortune and luck.

The author starts out by encouraging the individual to clear the slate of bitterness, hostility, resentment and jealousy. Getting rid of the little specks of pettiness will also help a lot. Then plan to fill each day with a generous mixture faith, patience, courage, work (without which the other ingredients are spoiled), hope, fidelity, generosity, kindness, rest, prayer, and meditation. Add a touch of fun, a dash of play and a cupful of good humor. Pour love into the whole mixture and mix with enthusiasm. Decorate with smiles and a sprinkling of joy, and then serve with cheerfulness and unselfishness. Following these directions for an entire year will inevitably increase your prospects for a truly successful life.

There is very little in this prescription about getting, taking, climbing to the top, my rights or other things that are the modern way to be successful. Jesus taught that if you want to get, you must give and before you can truly receive, you must give away.

#93 - STAYING POWER

Instant success is not always a blessing and failure is not always final. All of us desire to be successful and most of us want it from the first moment we try something. However, too much success too early can set us up for failure. We can become complacent and not be prepared for the changes that surely will come, because we think we have it made. While on the other hand failure, though disappointing, can better prepare us for we need to do. It helps keep us hungry and working. The one because of his fast start begins to coast, while the other one needs to work hard to gain momentum. Anything that is coasting soon comes to a stop.

Two young ball players started their major league careers on opening day in 1954, when the Cincinnati Reds played the Milwaukee Braves. Jim Greengrass seemed destined for greatness after hitting four doubles in his first major league game and leading Cincinnati to a 9-8 win. The other young man did not do so well. Hank Aaron started in left field for Milwaukee, but went 0 for 5 at the plate. Aaron's failure that day did not prove to be final. We don't know what impact that day had on his career, but he went on to hit more home runs than anyone else in the majors, including Babe Ruth.

Life is marathon, not a sprint. The Bible says that the prize goes to those who endure. Our goal in life should be to finish strong, not just doing well for a few years.

#94 - NO CARD FOR DAD

In the book **Father and Son** written by Gordon Dalby is a story about a Christian worker who ministered to inmates in the men's section of a prison. One of the inmates requested the worker to get a Mother's Day card for him so he could send it to his mother. The word quickly spread to the other prisoners and scores more requested cards. The Christian worker contacted a card company to see if they would be willing to supply cards to the prisoners. Before long, crates of cards arrived for the men to use.

The Mother's Day card idea had been so successful that the worker contacted the card company again to request cards for the men for Father's Day. Again, the company graciously responded with crates of cards suitable for the special day. Years later most of those cards were still in the crates. Few if any of the men in the prison chose to send a card to their dads.

One of the great tragedies of our day is the number of children who grow up without a father in the home who is a credible role model for his children. Many young boys do not have the privilege of a being guided by a loving dad who is firm, but fair. Many young ladies, all too early, go looking for love in the wrong place because they do not experienced proper love from the most important man in their young life - their father.

Jesus taught us to pray, "Our Father, who art in heaven" (Matthew 6:9). Our view of that heavenly Father is based primarily on our view of our earthly father.

#95 - SAYING NO TO A PARDON

Receiving a presidential pardon from execution would be welcome news - or so it would seem. Who would even think about turning it down? But such is the case that happened in 1830.

President Andrew Johnson issued a pardon from execution to George Wilson, who was to be hanged for robbing the United States mail. However, when word of the president's action reached Wilson, he refused the pardon. He said he wanted to be hanged.
Could Wilson do that? Could someone refuse a pardon?

The matter was referred to the Supreme Court for a decision. Chief Justice Marshall wrote the opinion for the court in which he stated that since a pardon is only a slip of paper, it is of no value until accepted. Yes, Wilson could refuse the pardon and the sentence must be carried out. Wilson was hanged.

Most of us shake our heads and wonder how anyone in their right mind could pass up such an offer. Why would anyone choose death over life? However, a pardon has been offered to all of us, but many refuse it. The Bible says we are to cast all our problems on God - but how many of us truly do that? Jesus also invites all who are weary and burdened to come to Him and He will give them rest, but still we try to drag on by ourselves. The greatest offer is the forgiveness of sins, but too often we try to atone for them by our own actions.

President Johnson must have been disappointed when his offer of clemency was refused. However, have you ever considered how God feels when we refuse His offers?

#96 - IS FAITH ENOUGH?

Several years ago skydiver, who was also a photographer, jumped out of a plane with a group of other skydivers in order to photograph their maneuvers. After filming the last parachute opening, the photographer reached for his own ripcord. To his surprise and alarm he did not have one. In his excitement and haste he had failed to put on his own chute and consequently plunged to his death.

We often hear people say, "It doesn't really matter what you believe as long as you believe." But that is not really true. The photographer believed in his parachute, but it wasn't buckled on. He, at first, was probably enjoying the jump. He thrilled to be able to share this moment with his buddies and couldn't wait to view the film. He had faith - but his faith let him down.

Faith in anything that cannot ultimately help us is useless. Our faith needs to be grounded in something or someone who has power to save us. Some of Jesus disciples marveled at one of His miracles. Jesus noticed their amazement and reminded them to "Have faith in God" (Mark 11:22). God, unlike the parachute, never becomes detached or unavailable when we need Him. At our times of greatest distress, He is always there. Faith in God will not disappoint us.

#97 - JEALOUSY

Two business owners had stores directly across the street from one another. A bitter rivalry grew between the two and daily they kept watch of each other's business to see how the other one was doing.

And angel appeared in a dream to one of the owners offering to grant a wish of his choosing. The only thing strange about the offer was that his competitor would get twice as much as he got. For example, if he asked for money, the man across the street would get twice as much. The same would go for honor, health, or whatever he wanted. The man thought for some time and then responded, "Make me blind in one eye!" Jealousy had gotten the best of him. When offered the prospect of blessing that could benefit both of them, he thought only of doubling the trouble to his neighbor.

One sign of jealousy is when we find it difficult to rejoice with those who rejoice. It is not hard to weep with those who weep, but when it comes to being truly happy for the success of a competitor, then that's another story.

How do we overcome these feelings of jealousy? How do we develop a right attitude? Conquering such feelings is not easy. However, we will be on our way to recovery, if we will concentrate on how God has blessed us rather than how much more someone else has.

#98 - DISCONTENT

Anthony Mellow writes about a disabled fox. He says,

> *"A man walking through the forest saw a fox that had lost its legs and wondered how it survived. Then he saw a tiger come in with game in its mouth. The tiger had his fill and left the rest of the meat for the fox. The next day God fed the fox by means of the same tiger. The man began to wonder at God's great goodness and said to himself, "I too shall just rest in a corner with full trust in the Lord and he will provide me with all I need." He did this for many days, but nothing happened and the poor fellow was almost at death's door when he heard a Voice say, 'O you who are in the path of error, open your eyes to the Truth! FOLLOW THE EXAMPLE OF THE TIGER and stop imitating the disabled fox.'"*

The Bible commends hard work and directs us to follow the industry of the ant. Gordon Graham says, "There are two kinds of discontent in this world: the discontent that gets to work and the discontent that wrings its hands. The first gets what it wants and the second loses what it has."   And Joseph Conrad said, "Lust for comfort is that stealthy thing that enters the house as a guest and then becomes a host and then a master."

#99 - GARBAGE IN

"Garbage in garbage out" is a rather old saying having to do with putting data into a computer. If the material put in is flawed, then it will come out the same way. There is also something to be said for what we put into our lives and minds. Parents often warn their children about the material they read, movies they watch and places they go, because they understand the power of outside influences.

A mother was standing at the kitchen sink peeling vegetables for the evening meal when her daughter asked to go with some of her friends to a place that had a bad reputation. As they discussed the matter the, the young teen said she recognized that it was a questionable place, but all the other girls were going and she didn't want to be left out." While they were talking, the mother picked up the vegetable peelings and began to put them into the salad. The daughter yelled at her mother and asked if she knew what she had just done. "Yes", the mother replied, "I know, but why?" "Why would you do that?" The mother replied, "Well, I decided that if you don't think that putting the garbage from the place you want to go won't affect your mind, then putting the garbage in the salad, won't affect our stomachs." The daughter got the picture and called her friends and told them she would not be going.

The Bible says, "Do not be misled: "Bad company corrupts good character" (I Corinthians 15:33).

#100 - MARRIAGE AND MONEY

Uncontrolled debt can be a cruel master that divides and often conquerors the best of marriages and relationships. One couple found their marriage on the verge of collapse because of the weight of debt. They were sick and tired of robbing Peter to pay Paul and pouring money into maintaining what they hadn't even paid for yet. In desperation they counseled with their Pastor who reminded them of a childhood slogan. He asked them to remember back to a grade school street crossing phrase that told them to stop-look-listen. As they discussed those three small words, they agreed that stop-look-listen had probably saved a lot of lives. He then asked them to consider three small questions to help them control their spending. Those three questions were, "Do I need it?" "Can I afford it?" "Can I live without it?"

All too frequently couples try to live beyond their means. They have too much month left over at the end of their money. Credit is often easy to obtain and soon the couple finds the depressing burden of trying to meet monthly obligations for bills incurred for things bought last year or the year before. Someone has estimated that approximately 90% of all family quarrels are over money or its misuse.

If you are deeply in debt and it is causing strife in your home, why not seek someone to give you good counsel. Also, ask yourself three simple questions before each purchase: "Do I need it?" "Can I afford it?" "Can I live without it?"

BIBLIOGRAPHY

#2 – Autoillustrator #4463, SF February 1989

#3 - Leadership Magazine, Vol XV, #4 Pg. 43 Fall 1994

#4 - Leadership Magazine Vol XVI #1 Pg 39, Winter 95)

#7 - **God at the Controls** by Jean Dye Johnson @1986 by New Tribes Mission, Sanford, FL.

#8 – Autoillustrator #4104, SF July 1984

#9 – Autoillustrator #4332 PE January 1989

#11 – Autoillustrator #4065 PE September 1988

#14 – Allen, Jon H., Ontario, CA in Leadership Magazine, 1984 Vol V, #2

#15 – Leadership Journal: Vol. XVI #1 Winter, 1995 Pg 38.

#16 - Newsletter from Greg and Julieann Allen, January 1995, Vol. 2 ISS. 1. Pioneer Mission Agency

#19 – Leadership Journal. Vol. XV #4 Fall 1994 Pg. 42.

#23 – Associated Press (March 1994) Submitted by Burford, Sherman L., Fairmont, WV

#24 – Autoillustrator #3957 SF June 1984.

#25 – Autoillustrator #4603 PE June 1989

#26 - Autoillustrator #4475 SF February 1989

#27 – Evinrude, Inc. History

#29 – Leadership Journal. Vol. XVI #1 Pg. 38 Winter 1995

#31 – Leadership Journal. Vol. XV, #4 Fall 1994

#32 – Autoillustrator # 4564,"PEMay89 QUALITY OF LIFE

#33 – Detroit News, Monday April 10, 1995 Pg. 1E

#35 – Illustration from Albert Mygatt.

#36 – Autoillustrator # 4037 PE August 1988

#37 - Autoillustrator # 4570 Sunday Sermons, Vol. 12, No. 4, July/August, 1982

#40 - Autoillustrator # 4386 PE February 1989

#41- Christian Clippings. May 1995 Pg. 28.

#43 - Autoillustrator #3883 PE June 1988.

#44 - Leadership Journal. Vol. 4. #4.

#47 - Leadership Journal. Vol. 4, #3.

#48 - Autoillustrator #4522 PE April 1989.

#49 - Leadership Journal. Vol. 4, #4.

#50 - Leadership Journal. Vol. 4, #2.

#53 - Autoillustrator #4352 PE January1989.

#55 – Knight, Walter B. Knight's Illustrations for Today.
Chicago: Moody Press, 1970, Pg 164.

#57 - Autoillustrator #3863 PE May 1988.

#58 – Illustration contributed by Zaida Chidester

#59 – Illustration contributed by Zaida Chidester

#60 - Autoillustrator #4166.

#61 - Autoillustrator #3864 PE May 1988.

#62 - Treasury of Illustrations, Wm B. Eerdmans Publishing
Company, Grand Rapids, 1963/

#65 - Hall, J. Walter Jr. Christian Clippings February 1990, Pg.
20.

#67 - Autoillustrator #3958 SF June 1984.

#69 - Autoillustrator #4189 PE October 1988.

#71 – Illustration contributed by Zaida Chidester

#73 - Autoillustrator #4964.

#74 – Insight. February 26, 1974.

#78 - Autoillustrator #4049 PE May 1988.

#79 - Knight, Walter B. Knight's Master Book of New
Illustrations.

#80 - Autoillustrator #4647 SF May 1989.

#81 – Infosearch #343.

#82 – Infosearch #1403.

#84 - Autoillustrator #12418 SF July 1993.

#85 – Christian Workers Magazine.

#87 - Infosearch #3 Character Assassination.

#88 - Autoillustrator #10588.

#89 - Infosearch #104.

#90 - Infosearch #145.

#91 - Autoillustrator #12855 SF December 1993.

#92 - Autoillustrator #5919.
#93 - Leadership Journal. Vol. 8 #3.
#94 –<u>Father and Son by Gordon </u>Dalby. Thomas Nelson Publishing, Nashville, TN. @ 1992.
#95 - Paokope. Baker Book House, P.O. Box 6287, Grand Rapids, MI 49516. A Quarerly flyer on preaching. April-June, 1997. Vol. 1, #2 Warren Wiersbe – Editor.
#96 - Autoillustrator #5358.
#97 - Autoillustrator #5078.
#98 – Autoillustrator #4196
#99 - Autoillustrator #4555 PE May 1989.
#100 - Illustration contributed by Barbara Wanner.